Hunter's cabin showing how projecting logs may be utilized.

SHELTERS, SHACKS AND SHANTIES

The Classic Guide to Building Wilderness Shelters

D. C. BEARD

with illustrations by the author

DOVER PUBLICATIONS, INC.
Mineola, New York

DEDICATED TO
DANIEL BARTLETT BEARD

BECAUSE OF HIS
LOVE OF THE BIG OUTDOORS

Bibliographical Note

This Dover edition, first published in 2004, is an unabridged republication of the work originally published in 1914 by Charles Scribner's Sons, New York.

Library of Congress Cataloging-in-Publication Data

Beard, Daniel Carter, 1850–1941.
    Shelters, shacks, and shanties : the classic guide to building wilderness shelters / D. C. Beard ; with illustrations by the author.
       p. cm.
    Originally published: Shelters, shacks, and shanties / Daniel Carter Beard. New York : Charles Scribner's Sons, 1914.
    ISBN-13: 978-0-486-43747-7 (pbk.)
    ISBN-10: 0-486-43747-7 (pbk.)
    1. Huts—Design and construction. 2. Log cabins—Design and construction. 3. Sheds—Design and construction. 4. Wilderness survival. I. Beard, Daniel Carter, 1850–1941. Shelters, shacks and shanties. II. Title.

TH4890.B4323 2004
613.6'9—dc22

2004052723

Manufactured in the United States by Courier Corporation
43747709   2013
www.doverpublications.com

FOREWORD

As this book is written for boys of all ages, it has been divided under two general heads, "The Tomahawk Camps" and "The Axe Camps," that is, camps which may be built with no tool but a hatchet, and camps that will need the aid of an axe.

The smallest boys can build some of the simple shelters and the older boys can build the more difficult ones. The reader may, if he likes, begin with the first of the book, build his way through it, and graduate by building the log houses; in doing this he will be closely following the history of the human race, because ever since our arboreal ancestors with prehensile toes scampered among the branches of the pre-glacial forests and built nestlike shelters in the trees, men have made themselves shacks for a temporary refuge. But as one of the members of the Camp-Fire Club of America, as one of the founders of the Boy Scouts of America, and as the founder of the Boy Pioneers of America, it would not be proper for the author to admit for one moment that there can be such a thing as a camp without a *camp-fire*, and for that reason the tree folks and the "missing link" whose remains were found in Java, and to whom the scientists gave the awe-inspiring name of Pithecanthropus erectus, cannot be counted as campers, because *they did not know how to build a camp-fire;* neither can we admit the ancient maker of stone implements, called eoliths, to be one of us, because he, too, knew not the joys of a camp-fire. But there was another fellow, called the Neanderthal man, who lived in the ice age in Europe and he *had* to be a camp-fire man or freeze! As far as we know, he was the first man to build a camp-fire. The cold weather made him hustle, and hustling developed him. True, he did cook and eat his neighbors once in a while, and even split their bones for the marrow; but we will forget that part and just remember him as the first camper in Europe.

Recently a pygmy skeleton was discovered near Los Angeles which is claimed to be about twenty thousand years old, but we do not know whether this man knew how to build a fire or not. We do know, however, that the American camper was here on this continent when our Bible was yet an unfinished manuscript and that he was building his fires, toasting his venison, and building "sheds" when the red-headed Eric settled in Greenland, when Thorwald fought with the "Skraelings," and Biarni's dragon ship made the trip down the coast of Vineland about the dawn of the Christian era. We also know that the American camper was here when Columbus with his comical toy ships was blundering around the West Indies. We also know that the American camper watched Henry Hudson steer the *Half Moon* around Manhattan Island. It is this same American camper who has taught us to build many of the shacks to be found in the following pages.

The shacks, sheds, shanties, and shelters described in the following pages are, all of them, similar to those used by the people on this continent or suggested by the ones in use and are typically American; and the designs are suited to the arctics, the tropics, and temperate climes; also to the plains, the mountains, the desert, the bog, and even the water.

It seems to be natural and proper to follow the camp as it grows until it develops into a somewhat pretentious log house, but this book must not be considered as competing in any manner with professional architects. The buildings here suggested require a woodsman more than an architect; the work demands more the skill of the axeman than that of the carpenter and joiner. The log houses are supposed to be buildings which any real outdoor man should be able to erect by himself and for himself. Many of the buildings have already been built in many parts of the country by Boy Pioneers and Boy Scouts.

This book is not intended as an encyclopedia or history of primitive architecture; the bureaus at Washington, and the Museum of Natural History, are better equipped for that purpose than the author.

The boys will undoubtedly acquire a dexterity and skill in building the shacks and shanties here described, which will be of lasting benefit to them whether they acquire the skill by building camps "just for the fun of the thing" or in building them for the more practical purpose of furnishing shelter for overnight pleasure hikes, for the wilderness trail, or for permanent camps while living in the open.

It has been the writer's experience that the readers depend more upon his diagrams than they do upon the written matter in his books, and so in this book he has again attempted to make the diagrams self-explanatory. The book was written in answer to requests by many people interested in the Boy Scout movement and others interested in the general activities of boys, and also in answer to the personal demands of hundreds of boys and many men.

The drawings are all original and many of them invented by the author himself and published here for the first time, for the purpose of supplying all the boy readers, the Boy Scouts, and other older "boys," calling themselves Scoutmasters and sportsmen, with practical hints, drawings, and descriptions showing how to build suitable shelters for temporary or permanent camps.

DANIEL CARTER BEARD.

FLUSHING, LONG ISLAND,
    APRIL 1, 1914.

CONTENTS

ix

Contents   xi

SHELTERS, SHACKS, AND SHANTIES

I

WHERE TO FIND MOUNTAIN GOOSE. HOW TO PICK AND USE ITS FEATHERS

It may be necessary for me to remind the boys that they must use the material at hand in building their shacks, shelters, sheds, and shanties, and that they are very fortunate if their camp is located in a country where the mountain goose is to be found.

The Mountain Goose

From Labrador down to the northwestern borders of New England and New York and from thence to southwestern Virginia, North Carolina, and Tennessee, the woodsman and camper may make their beds from the feathers of the "mountain goose." The mountain goose is also found inhabiting the frozen soil of Alaska and following the Pacific and the Rocky Mountains the Abies make their dwelling-place as far south as Guatemala. Consequently, the Abies, or mountain goose, should be a familiar friend of all the scouts who live in the mountainous country, north, south, east, and west.

1

Sapin—Cho-kho-tung

I forgot to say that the mountain goose (Figs. 1 and 2) is not a bird but a tree. It is humorously called a goose by the woodsmen because they all make their beds of its "feathers." It is the *sapin* of the French-Canadians, the *cho-kho-tung* of the New York Indians, the balsam of the tenderfoot, the Christmas-tree of the little folk, and that particular Coniferæ known by the dry-as-dust botanist as Abies. There is nothing in nature which has a wilder, more sylvan and charming perfume than the balsam, and the scout who has not slept in the woods on a balsam bed has a pleasure in store for him.

Balsam

The leaves of the balsam are blunt or rounded at the ends and some of them are even dented or notched in place of being sharp-pointed. Each spine or leaf is a scant one inch in length and very flat; the upper part is grooved and of a dark bluish-green color. The under-side is much lighter, often almost silvery white. The balsam blossoms in April or May, and the fruit or cones stand upright on the branches. These vary from two to four inches in length. The balsam-trees are seldom large, not many of them being over sixty feet high with trunks from one to less than three feet through. The bark on the trunks is gray in color and marked with horizontal rows of blisters. Each of these contains a small, sticky sap like glycerine. Fig. 1 shows the cone and leaves of one of the Southern balsams known as the she-balsam, and Fig. 2 shows the celebrated balsam-fir tree of the north country, cone and branch.

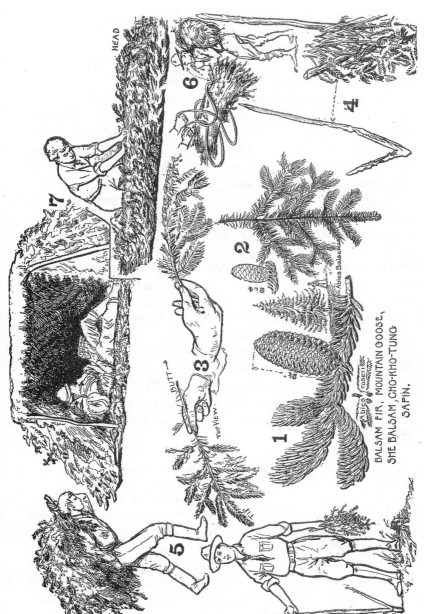

BALSAM FIR, MOUNTAIN GOOSE,
SHE BALSAM, CHO-KHO-TUNG
SAPIN.

Showing the use of the mountain goose.

Balsam Beds

The balsam bed is made of the small twigs of balsam-trees. In gathering these, collect twigs of different lengths, from eighteen inches long (to be used as the foundation of the bed) to ten or twelve inches long (for the top layer). If you want to rest well, do not economize on the amount you gather; many a time I have had my bones ache as a result of being too tired to make my bed properly and attempting to sleep on a thin layer of boughs.

If you attempt to chop off the boughs of balsam they will resent your effort by springing back and slapping you in the face. You can cut them with your knife, but it is slow work and will blister your hands. Take twig by twig with the thumb and fingers (the thumb on top, pointing toward the tip of the bough, and the two forefingers underneath); press down with the thumb, and with a twist of the wrist you can snap the twigs like pipe-stems. Fig. 3 shows two views of the hands in a proper position to snap off twigs easily and clean. The one at the left shows the hand as it would appear looking down upon it; the one at the right shows the view as you look at it from the side.

Packing Boughs

After collecting a handful of boughs, string them on a stick which you have previously prepared (Fig. 4). This stick should be of strong, green hardwood, four or five feet long with a fork about six inches long left on it at the butt end to keep the boughs from sliding off, and sharpened at the upper end so that it can be easily poked through a handful of boughs. String the boughs on this stick as you would string fish, but do it one handful at a time, allowing the butts to point in different directions.

It is astonishing to see the amount of boughs you can carry when strung on a stick in this manner and thrown over your shoulder as in Fig. 5. If you have a lash rope, place the boughs on a loop of the rope, as in Fig. 6, then bring the two ends of the rope up through the loop and sling the bundle on your back.

Clean Your Hands

When you have finished gathering the material for your bed your hands will be covered with a sticky sap, and, although they will be a sorry sight, a little lard or baking grease will soften the pitchy substance so that it may be washed off with soap and water.

How to Make Beds

To make your bed, spread a layer of the larger boughs on the ground; commence at the head and shingle them down to the foot so that the tips point toward the head of the bed, overlapping the butts (Fig. 7). Continue this until your mattress is thick enough to make a soft couch upon which you can sleep as comfortably as you do at home. Cover the couch with one blanket and use the bag containing your coat, extra clothes, and sweater for a pillow. Then if you do not sleep well, you must blame the cook.

Other Bedding

If you should happen to be camping in a country destitute of balsam, hemlock, or pine, you can make a good spring mattress by collecting small green branches of any sort of tree which is springy and elastic. Build the mattress as already described. On top of this put a thick layer of hay, straw, or dry leaves or even green material, provided you have a rubber blanket or poncho to cover the latter. In Kentucky I have made a mattress of this description and covered the branches with a thick layer of the purple blossoms of ironweed; over this I spread a rubber army blanket to keep out the moisture from the green stuff and on top of this made my bed with my other blankets. It was as comfortable a couch as I have ever slept on; in fact, it was literally a bed of flowers.

II

THE HALF-CAVE SHELTER

THE first object of a roof of any kind is protection against the weather; no shelter is necessary in fair weather unless the sun in the day or the dampness or coolness of the night cause discomfort. In parts of the West there is so little rain that a tent is often an unnecessary burden, but in the East and the other parts of the country some sort of shelter is necessary for health and comfort.

The original American was always quick to see the advantages offered by an overhanging cliff for a camp site (Figs. 9, 10). His simple camps all through the arid Southwest had gradually turned into carefully built houses long before we came here. The overhanging cliffs protected the buildings from the rain and weather, and the site was easily defended from enemies. But while these cliff-dwellings had reached the dignity of castles in the Southwest, in the Eastern States—Pennsylvania, for instance—the Iroquois Indians were making primitive camps and using every available overhanging cliff for that purpose.

To-day any one may use a pointed stick on the floor of one of these half caves and unearth, as I have done, numerous potsherds, mussel shells, bone awls, flint arrowheads, split bones of large game animals, and the burnt wood of centuries of camp-fires which tell the tale of the first lean-to shelter used by camping man in America.

Half Caves

The projecting ledges of bluestone that have horizontal seams form half caves from the falling apart of the lower layers of the cliff caused by rain and ice and often aided by the fine roots of the black birch, rock oak, and other plants, until nature has worked long enough as a quarry-man and produced half caves large enough to shelter a stooping man (Figs. 8, 9, and 10).

Although not always necessary, it is sometimes best to make a shelter for the open face of such a cave, even if we only need it for a temporary camp (Fig. 10); this may be done by resting poles slanting against the face of the cliff and over these making a covering of balsam, pine, hemlock, palmetto, palm branches, or any available material for thatch to shed the rain and prevent it driving under the cliff to wet our bedding.

Walls

It is not always necessary to thatch the wall; a number of green boughs with leaves adhering may be rested against the cliffs and will answer for that purpose. Set the boughs upside down so that they will shed the rain and not hold it so as to drip into camp. Use your common sense and gumption, which will teach you that all the boughs should point downward and not upward as most of them naturally grow. I am careful to call your attention to this because I lately saw some men teaching Boy Scouts how to make camps and they were placing the boughs for the lads around the shelter with their branches pointing upward in such a manner that they could not shed the rain. These instructors were city men and apparently thought that the boughs were for no other purpose than to give privacy to the occupants of the shelter,

The half-cave shelter.

forgetting that in the wilds the wilderness itself furnishes privacy.

The half cave was probably the first lean-to or shelter in this country, but overhanging cliffs are not always found where we wish to make our camp and we must resort to other forms of shelter and the use of other material in such localities.

III

HOW TO MAKE THE FALLEN-TREE SHELTER AND THE SCOUT-MASTER

Now that you know how to make a bed in a half cave, we will take up the most simple and primitive manufactured shelters.

Fallen-Tree Shelter

For a one-man one-night stand, select a thick-foliaged fir-tree and cut it partly through the trunk so that it will fall as shown in Fig. 11; then trim off the branches on the under-side so as to leave room to make your bed beneath the branches; next trim the branches off the top or roof of the trunk and with them thatch the roof. Do this by setting the branches with their butts up as shown in the right-hand shelter of Fig. 13, and then thatch with smaller browse as described in making the bed. This will make a cosey one-night shelter.

The Scout-Master

Or take three forked sticks (*A*, *B*, and *C*, Fig. 12), and interlock the forked ends so that they will stand as shown in Fig. 12. Over this framework rest branches with the butt ends up as shown in the right-hand shelter (Fig. 13), or lay a number of poles as shown in the left-hand figure (Fig. 12) and thatch this with browse as illustrated by the left-hand shelter in Fig. 13, or take elm, spruce, or birch bark and shingle as in Fig. 14. These shelters may be built for one boy or they may be made large enough for several men. They may be thatched with balsam, spruce, pine, or hemlock boughs, or with cat-tails, rushes (see Figs. 66 and 69) or any kind of long-stemmed weeds or palmetto leaves.

To Peel Bark

In the first place, I trust that the reader has enough common sense and sufficient love of the woods to prevent him from killing or marring and disfiguring trees where trees are not plenty, and this restriction includes all settled or partially settled parts of the country. But in the real forests and wilderness, miles and miles away from human habitation, there are few campers and consequently there will be fewer trees injured, and these few will not be missed.

Selecting Bark

To get the birch bark, select a tree with a smooth trunk devoid of branches and, placing skids for the trunk to fall upon (Fig. 38), fell the tree (see Figs. 112, 113, 114, 115, 116, 117, and 118), and then cut a circle around the trunk at the two ends of the log and a slit from one circle clean up to the other circle (Fig. 38); next, with a sharp stick shaped like a blunt-edged chisel, pry off the bark carefully until you take the piece off in one whole section. If it is spruce bark or any other bark you seek, hunt through the woods for a comparatively smooth trunk and proceed in the same manner as with the birch. To take it off a standing tree, cut one circle down at the butt and another as high as you can reach (Fig. 118) and slit it along a perpendicular line connecting the two cuts as in Fig. 38.

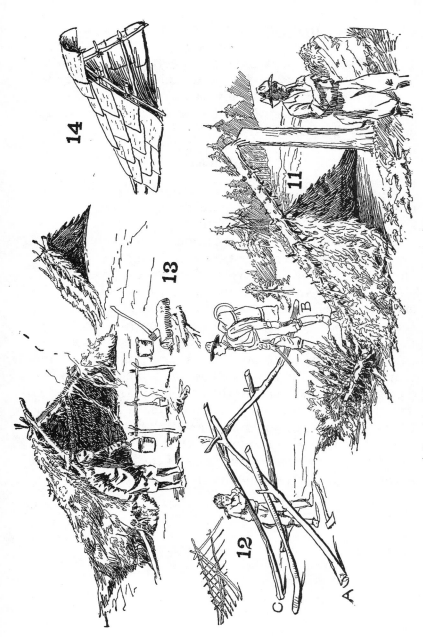

One-night shelter. The fallen tree and the scout-master.

This will doubtless in time kill the tree, but far from human habitations the few trees killed in this manner may do the forest good by giving more room for others to grow.   Near town or where the forests are small use the bark from the old dead trees.

Using Bark

To shingle with bark, cut the bark in convenient sec tions, commence at the bottom, place one piece of bark set on edge flat against the wall of your shelter, place a piece of bark next to it in the same manner, allowing the one edge to overlap the first piece a few inches, and so on all the way around your shack; then place a layer of bark above this in the same manner as the first one, the end edges overlapping, the bottom edges also overlapping the first row three or four inches or even more.   Hold these pieces of bark in place by stakes driven in the ground against them or poles laid over them, according to the shape or form of your shelter.   Continue thus to the comb of the roof, then over the part where the bark of the sides meets on the top lay another layer of bark covering the crown, ridge, comb, or apex and protecting it from the rain.   In the wigwam-shaped shelters, or rather I should say those of teepee form, the point of the cone or pyramid is left open to serve as chimney for smoke to escape.

IV

HOW TO MAKE THE ADIRONDACK, THE WICK-UP, THE BARK TEEPEE, THE PIONEER, AND THE SCOUT

The Adirondack

THE next shelter is what is generally known as the Adirondack shelter, which is a lean-to open in the front like a "Baker" or a "Dan Beard" tent. Although it is popularly called the Adirondack camp, it antedates the time when the Adirondacks were first used as a fashionable resort. Daniel Boone was wont to make such a camp in the forests of Kentucky. The lean-to or Adirondack camp is easily made and very popular. Sometimes two of them are built facing each other with an open space between for the camp-fire. But the usual manner is to set up two uprights as in Fig. 15, then lay a crosspiece through the crotches and rest poles against this crosspiece (Fig. 16). Over these poles other poles are laid horizontally and the roof thatched with browse by the method shown by Fig. 6, but here the tips of the browse must point down and be held in place by other poles (Fig. 10) on top of it. Sometimes a log is put at the bottom of the slanting poles and sometimes more logs are placed as shown in Figs. 15 and 16 and the space between them floored with balsam or browse.

The Scout

Where birch bark is obtainable it is shingled with slabs of this bark as already described, and as shown in Fig. 17,

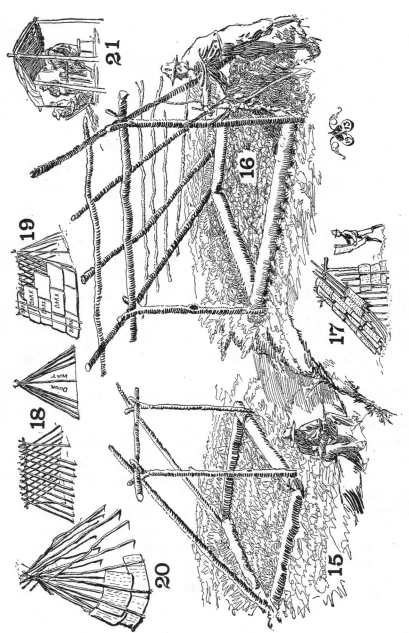

The Adirondack. The scout, the pioneer, and the bark teepee.

the bark being held in place on the roof by poles laid over it and on the side by stakes being driven in the ground outside of the bark to hold it in place as in Fig. 17.

The Pioneer

Fig. 18 shows the Pioneer, a tent form of shack, and Fig. 19 shows how the bark is placed like shingles overlapping each other so as to shed the rain. The doorway of the tent shack is made by leaning poles against forked sticks, their butts forming a semicircle in front, or rather the arc of a circle, and by bracing them against the forked stick fore and aft they add stability to the structure.

Bark Teepee

Or you may, if you choose, lash three sticks together at the top ends, spread them in the form of a tripod, then lay other sticks against them, their butts forming a circle in the form of a teepee (Fig. 20).

Commence at the bottom as you do in shingling a roof and place sections of birch bark around, others above them overlapping them, and hold them in place by resting poles against them. If your camp is to be occupied for a week or so, it may be convenient to build a wick-up shelter as a dining-room like the one shown in Fig. 21. This is made with six uprights, two to hold the ridge-pole and two to hold the eaves, and may be shingled over with browse or birch, elm, spruce, or other bark; shingle with the browse in the same manner as that described for the bark, beginning at the eaves and allowing each row of browse to overlap the butts of the one below it.

V

HOW TO MAKE BEAVER-MAT HUTS OR FAGOT SHACKS WITHOUT INJURY TO THE TREES

Material

IN building a shelter use every and any thing handy for the purpose; ofttimes an uprooted tree will furnish a well-made adobe wall, where the spreading roots have torn off the surface soil as the tree fell and what was the under-side is now an exposed wall of clay, against which you may rest the poles for the roof of a lean-to. Or the side of the cliff (Fig. 23) may offer you the same opportunity. Maybe two or three trees will be found willing to act as uprights (Fig. 24). Where you use a wall of any kind, rock, roots, or bank, it will, of course, be necessary to have your door-way at one side of the shack as in Fig. 23. The upright poles may be on stony ground where their butts cannot well be planted in the earth, and there it will be necessary to brace them with slanting poles (Fig. 25). Each camp will offer problems of its own, problems which add much to the interest and pleasure of camp making.

Beaver Mat

The beaver-mat camp is a new one and, under favor-able conditions, a good one. Cut your poles the length required for the framework of the sides, lash them to-gether with the green rootlets of the tamarack or strips of bark of the papaw, elm, cedar, or the inside bark of the

18

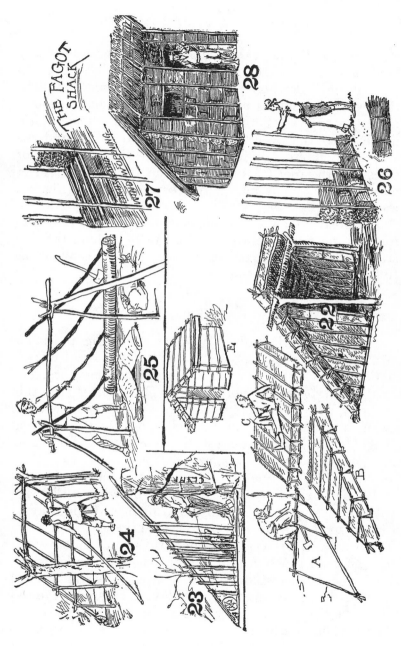

Shelters adapted to conditions. The beaver-mat and the fagot shack.

chestnut (*A*, Fig. 22); then make a bed of browse of any kind handy, but make it in the manner described for making balsam beds (Fig. 7). You will, of course, thatch so that when the side is erected it is shingled like a house, the upper rows overlapping the lower ones. Then lash a duplicate frame over the browse-padded frame and the side is complete (*B*, Fig. 22). Make the other side or sides and the roof (*C*, Fig. 22) in the same manner, after which it is a simple matter to erect your shack (Fig. 22, and *E*, Fig. 22).

The great advantage of this sort of shelter is that it is much easier to do your thatching on the ground than on standing walls, and also, when done, it is so compact as to be practically water-proof.

Fagot Shack

The fagot shack is also a new style of camp and is intended for use in places where large timber cannot be cut, but where dwarf willows, bamboo cane, alders, or other small underbrush is more or less plentiful. From this gather a plentiful supply of twigs and with improvised twine bind the twigs into bundles of equal size. Use these bundles as you would stones in building the wall and lay them so as to break joints, that is, so that the joints are never in a continuous line. Hold the wall in place by stakes as shown in Fig. 26. Use the browse, small twigs with the leaves adhering to them, in place of mortar or cement so as to level your bundles and prevent their rocking on uneven surfaces. The doorways and window openings offer no problem that a rank outsider cannot solve. Fig. 27 shows the window opening, also shows you how the window-sill can be made firm by laying rods over the top of the fagots. Rods are also used across the top of the doorway upon which to place the bundles of fagots or twigs. Twigs is probably the best term to use here, as fagots might be thought to mean larger sticks, which may be stiff and obstinate and hard to handle.

Roofs

After the walls are erected, a beaver-mat roof may be placed upon them or a roof made on a frame such as shown in Fig. 28 and thatched with small sticks over which a thatch of straw, hay, rushes (Figs. 66 and 69), or browse may be used to shed the rain.

One great advantage which recommends the beaver-mat and fagot camp to lovers of nature and students of forestry lies in the fact that it is unnecessary to cut down or destroy a single large or valuable young tree in order to procure the material necessary to make the camp. Both of these camps can be made in forest lands by using the lower branches of the trees, which, when properly cut close to the trunk (Fig. 121), do not injure the standing timber. The fagot hut may be made into a permanent camp by plastering the outside with soft mud or clay and treating the inside walls in the same manner, thus transforming it into an adobe shack.

VI

INDIAN SHACKS AND SHELTERS

WHILE the ingenuity of the white man may make improvements upon the wick-ups, arbors, huts, and shelters of the native red man, we must not forget that these native shelters have been used with success by the Indians for centuries, also we must not forget that our principal objection to many of them lies in the fact that they are ill ventilated and dirty, both of which defects may be remedied without materially departing from the lines laid down by the savage architects. The making of windows will supply ventilation to Indian huts, but the form of the hut we must bear in mind is made to suit the locality in which we find it.

Apache Hogan

The White Mountain Apache builds a tent-shaped shack (Figs. 29 and 32) which is practically the same as that already described and shown in Figs. 18 and 19, the difference being that the Apache shack is not covered with birch bark, a material peculiar to the North, but the Apache uses a thatch of the rank grass to be found where his shacks are located. To-day, however, the White Mountain Apache has become so degenerate and so lost to the true sense of dignity as a savage that he stoops to use corn-stalks with which to thatch the long, sloping sides of his shed-like house· but by so doing he really shows

22

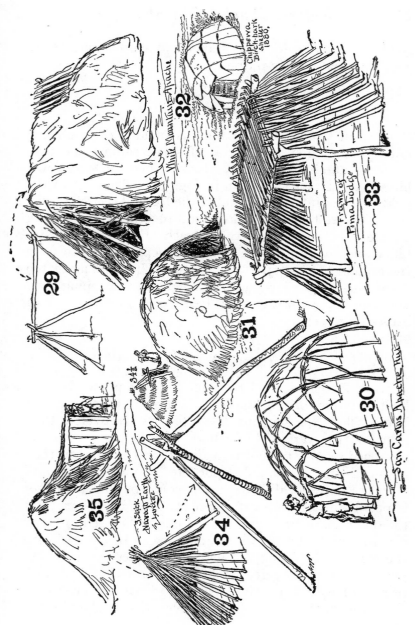

29

32

Chippewa
Birch-bark
Saguart
1880,

White Mountain Apache

33

Frame of
Pima Lodge

31

30

San Carlos Apache Hut

34½

35

3.Sack
Navajo Earth
Lodge

34

Designs adapted from Indian models.

good horse sense, for corn-stalks and corn leaves make good material for the purpose.

San Carlos Shack

The San Carlos Apache Indians build a dome-shaped hut by making a framework of small saplings bent in arches as the boys did in Kentucky when the writer was himself a lad, and as shown in Fig. 30. The ends of the pole are sunk into the ground in the form of a circle, while their tips are bent over and bound together thus forming a series of loops which overlap each other and give stability and support to the principal loops which run from the ground to the top of the dome. The Indians thatch these huts with bear-grass arranged in overlapping rows and held in place with strings (see Fig. 69) made of yucca leaves (Fig. 31).

Chippewa Shack

Much farther north I have seen the Chippewa Indians build a framework in practically the same manner as the San Carlos Apache, but the Chippewas covered their frame with layers of birch bark held in place by ropes stretched over it as shown in Fig. 32. The door to their huts consisted of a blanket portière.

In the same locality to-day it would be difficult if not impossible to procure such large strips of birch bark; but the dome-shaped frame is a good one to be used in many localities and, like all other frames, it can be covered with the material at hand. It may be shingled with smaller pieces of bark, covered with brush and thatched with browse or with hay, straw, palmetto leaves, palm leaves, or rushes, or it may be plastered over with mud and made an adobe hut.

Pima Lodge

The Pima Indians make a flat-roofed lodge with slanting walls (Fig. 33) which may be adapted for our use in almost any section of the country. It can be made warm and tight for the far North and cool and airy for the arid regions of the Southwest. The framework, as you may see by referring to the diagram, is similar to the wick-ups we men made when we were boys, and which are described in the "American Boy's Handy Book," consisting of four upright posts supporting in their crotches two crosspieces over which a flat roof is made by placing poles across. But the sides of this shack are not upright but made by resting leaning poles against the eaves.

White Man's Walls

The principal difference between a white man's architecture and the Indian's lies in the fact that the white man, with brick, stone, or frame house in his mind, is possessed of a desire to build perpendicular walls—walls which are hard to thatch and difficult to cover with turf, especially in the far North, where there is no true sod such as we understand in the middle country, where our grass grows thickly with interlacing roots. Boys will do well to remember this and imitate the Indian in making slanting walls for their shacks, shanties, and shelters in the woods. If they have boards or stone or brick or logs with which to build they may, with propriety, use a perpendicular wall. The Pima Indians, according to Pliny Earle Goddard, associate curator of anthropology of the American Museum of Natural History, thatch their houses with arrow brush and not infrequently bank the sides of the shack with dirt.

Adobe Roof

If you want to put a dirt roof on a shack of this description, cover the poles with small boughs or browse, green or dry leaves, straw, hay, grass, or rushes and put the sod over the top of this. If in place of making the roof flat as shown in Fig. 33, you slant it so as to shed the rain, this 'ort of shack will do for almost any climate, but with a flat roof it is only fitted for the arid country or for a shelter from the sun when it is not expected to be used during the rain.

Navajo

The teepee-shaped hut used by the Navajo Indians *will* shed the rain. To build this shack interlock three forked sticks as shown in the diagram, then lay other poles up against the forks of these sticks so that the butts of the poles will form a circle on the ground (Fig. 34). Thatch this with any material handy, after which you may cover it with dirt as the Navajos do, in which case you had better build a hallway for entrance, as shown in Fig. 35. This same teepee form is used by the California Indians and thatched with wild hay (Fig. 34½).

VII

BIRCH BARK OR TAR PAPER SHACK

A DESCRIPTION of the Pontiac was first published in my "Field and Forest Handy Book," a book which contains several shelters similar to the ones here given, most of which were originally made for Caspar Whitney while he was editor of *Outing*.

The Pontiac

The Pontiac, as here given, is my own design and invention (Fig. 36). It is supposed to be shingled with birch bark, but, as is the case with all these camps, other bark may be substituted for the birch, and, if no bark is within reach and you are near enough to civilization, tar paper makes an excellent substitute. Fig. 37 shows the framework of a Pontiac with a ridge-pole, but the ridge-pole is not necessary and the shack may be built without it, as shown in Figs. 36 and 39, where the rafter poles rest upon the two side-plates over which they project to form the apex of the roof. In Fig. 39, although the side-plates are drawn, the rafter or roof poles are not because the diagram is supposed to be a sort of X-ray affair to show the internal construction. The opening for smoke need not be more than half as large as it is in Fig. 39 and it may be covered up in inclement weather with a piece of bark so as to keep out the rain.

Cutting Bark

Fig. 38 shows a tree felled in order to procure bark. You will note that the bark is cut round at the bottom and at the top and a slit is made connecting the two cuts as already described so that the bark may be peeled off by running a blunt instrument or a stick, whittled to the shape of a paper-cutter or dull chisel, under the edge of the bark and carefully peeling it back. If it is necessary to "tote" the bark any distance over the trail, Fig. 38 shows how to roll it up and how to bind the roll with cord or rope so that it may be slung on the back as the man is "toting" it in Fig. 36.

Building the Pontiac

To build a Pontiac, first erect the uprights *E* and *E*, Fig. 37, then the other two similar uprights at the rear and lay the side-plates *G* in the forks of the uprights; next erect the upright *H* and one in the rear to correspond, and across this lay the ridge-pole. Next take a couple of logs and put them at the foot of the *E* poles, or, if you want more room, further back toward where the roof poles *F* will come. Place one of these logs on top of the other as shown in Figs. 36 and 39. Keep them in place by driving sticks on each side of them. Put two more logs upon the other side of the Pontiac and then lay your roof poles or rafters up against the side-plates and over the logs as shown in diagrams 36, 37, and 39. Fig. 36 shows the roof partially shingled and the sides partially covered, so that you may better understand how it is done.

Shingling with Bark

Commence at the bottom and lay the first row with the edges overlapping for walls; for the roof you may lay

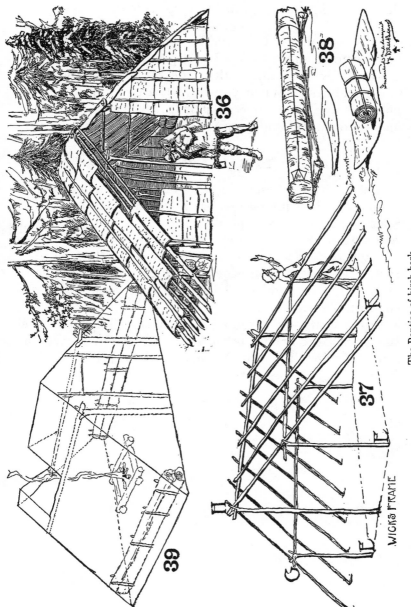

The Pontiac of birch bark.

one row of shingles from the bottom up to the ridge and hold them in place by resting a pole on them; then lay the next row of shingles alongside by slipping the edges under the first. When you have the two sides covered, put bark over the ridge as shown in Fig. 36. This will make a beautiful and comfortable little camp.

To Keep Out Cold

Built as here described, the cold wind might come through in the winter-time, but if you can gather a lot of Sphagnum moss from the nearest swamp and cover your roof with it and then shingle that over with another layer of birch bark, the cold wind will not come through your roof. If you treat your side walls in the same manner and heap dirt up around the edges of them, you will have a comfortable winter camp.

In the winter-time you will find it very difficult to peel the birch bark or any other kind of bark, but when the sap is flowing it is not so difficult to secure bark slabs from many varieties of trees.

VIII

INDIAN COMMUNAL HOUSES

WHEN the French Communists were raising Cain in Europe they doubtless thought their idea was practically new, but thousands of years before they bore the red banner through the streets of Paris the American Indians were living quiet and peaceful communal lives on this continent; when I use the words *quiet* and *peaceful*, I, of course, mean as regards their own particular commune and not taking into account their attitude toward their neighbors. The Pueblo Indians built themselves adobe communal houses, the Nez Percés built themselves houses of sticks and dry grass one hundred and fifty feet long sometimes, containing forty-eight families, while the Nechecolles had houses two hundred and twenty-six feet in length! But this is not a book of history; all we want to know is how to build shacks for our own use; so we will borrow one from the communal home of the Iroquois. It is not necessary for us to make this one hundred feet long, as the Iroquois Indians did. We can make a diminutive one as a playhouse for our children, a moderate-sized one as a camp for our Boy Scouts, or a good-sized one for a party of full-grown campers.

But first we must gather a number of long, flexible saplings and plant them in two rows with their butt ends in the ground, as shown in Fig. 40, after which we may bend their upper ends so that they will overlap each other and form equal-sized arches, when they are lashed together,

31

with twine if we have it, or with wire if it is handy; but if we are real woodsmen, we will bind them with rope made of fibres of bark or the flexible roots which we find in the forests. Then we bind horizontal poles or rods to the arches, placing the poles about a foot or two apart according to the material with which we are to shingle it. We make a simple doorway with upright posts at one end and bind the horizontal posts on as we did at the sides. Next we shingle it with bark or with strips of tar paper and hold the shingles in place by binding poles upon the outside, as shown in Fig. 41. A hole or holes are left in the roof over the fireplaces for openings for the smoke to escape. In lieu of a chimney a wind-shield of bark is fastened at its lower edge by pieces of twine to the roof so as to shield the opening; this wind-shield should be movable so that it may be shifted according to the wind. The Iroquois is an easily constructed shelter, useful to man, and one which will delight the heart of the Boy Scouts or any other set of boys.

The Pawnee Hogan

The Pawnee hogan is usually covered with sod or dirt, but it may be covered with bark, with canvas, or thatched with straw or with browse, as the camper may choose. Fig. 42 shows the framework in the skeleton form. The rafter poles are placed wigwam fashion and should be very close together in the finished structure; so also should be the short sticks forming the side walls and the walls to the hallway or entrance. To build this hogan, first erect a circle of short forked sticks, setting their ends firmly in the ground. Inside of this erect four longer forked sticks, then place across these four horizontal side-plates, or maybe they might be more properly called "purlins," in which case the sticks laid on the forks of the circle of small

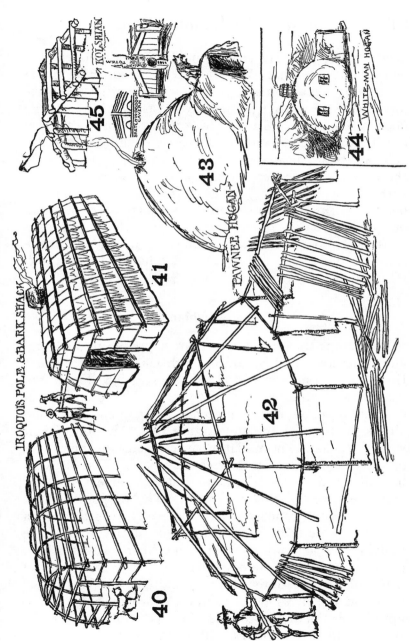

The Iroquois, the Pawnee hogan, the white man's hogan, and the kolshian

uprights will properly correspond to the side-plates of a
white man's dwelling. After the circle and square (Fig. 42)
have been erected, make your doorway with two short-
forked sticks and your hallway by sticks running from the
door to side-plates. In thatching your roof or in covering
it with any sort of material, leave an opening at the top
(Fig. 43) to act as a chimney for your centre camp-fire. If
the roof is to be covered with sod or adobe, cover it first
with browse, hay, straw, or rushes, making a thick mattress
over the entire structure. On top of this plaster your mud
or sod (Fig. 43). If you intend to use this hogan as a
more or less permanent camp you can put windows in the
sides to admit light and air and use a hollow log or a barrel for a chimney as shown in Fig. 44.

The Kolshian

The camps thus far described are supposed to be "tomahawk camps," that is, camps which may be built without
the use of a lumberman's axe. The kolshian (Fig. 45) of
Alaska, when built by the natives, is a large communal
council-house, but I have placed it here among the "tomahawk camps" on the supposition that some one might
want to build one in miniature as a novelty on their place
or as a council-room for their young scouts. The Alaskans
hew all the timber out by hand, but, of course, the reader
may use sawed or milled lumber. The proper entrance
to a kolshian or rancheree, as Elliot calls it, is through a
doorway made in the huge totem-pole at the front of the
building. The roof is covered with splits or shakes held in
place by poles laid across them, the sides are made of
hewn planks set upright, and the front has two heavy
planks at the eaves which run down through holes in two
upright planks at the corners (Fig. 45). These with the
sill plank bind the upright wall planks in place.

The kolshian is undoubtedly a very ancient form of building and may be related to the houses built by the ancient cavemen of Europe. The first human house-builders are said to belong to the Cro-Magnon race who lived in caves in the winter-time, and on the walls of one of the caverns (Dordogne cavern) some Cro-Magnon budding architect made a rough sketch of one of their houses (middle sketch, Fig. 45). When you compare the house with the kolshian the resemblance is very striking, and more so when we remember that the kolshian floor is underground, indicating that it is related to or suggested by a natural cavern.

IX

BARK AND TAR PAPER

To further illustrate the use of bark and tar paper, I have made the sketches shown by Figs. 46, 47, and 48. Fig. 47 is a log shack with an arched roof drawn from a photograph in my collection. To keep the interior warm not only the roof but the sides of the house as well have been shingled with bark, leaving only the ends of the logs protruding to tell of what material the house is really constructed. Fig. 47 shows a fisherman's hut made with a few sticks and bark. Fig. 48 shows a tar paper camp, that is, a camp where everything is covered with tar paper in place of bark. The house is made with a skeleton of poles on which the tar paper is tacked, the kitchen is an open shed with tar paper roof, and even the table is made by covering the cross sticks shown in the diagram with sheets of tar paper in place of the birch bark usually used for that purpose.

Personally I do not like tar paper; it seems to rob the camp of a true flavor of the woods; it knocks the sentiment out of it, and, except to sailors, the odor of the tar is not nearly as delightful as that of the fragrant balsam boughs. Nevertheless, tar paper is now used in all the lumber camps and is spreading farther and farther into the woods as the birch bark becomes scarce and the "tote-roads" are improved.

When one can enter the woods with an automobile, you must expect to find tar paper camps, because the paper is

Showing use of bark and tar paper.

easily transported, easily handled, and easily applied for the purpose of the camper.

Practically any form of tent may be reproduced by tacking tar paper to sticks arranged in the proper manner, but if you make a wigwam of tar paper, do paint it red, green, or yellow, or whitewash it; do anything which will take off the civilized, funereal look of the affair.

X

A SAWED-LUMBER SHANTY

BEFORE we proceed any further it may be best to give
the plan of a workshop, a camp, an outhouse, or a shed
to be made of sawed lumber, the framework of which is
made of what is known as two-by-fours, that is, pieces
of lumber two inches thick by four inches wide. The plans
used here are from my book "The Jack of All Trades,"
but the dimensions may be altered to suit your convenience. The sills, which are four inches by four inches, are
also supposed to be made by nailing two two-by-fours together. First stake out your foundation and see that the
corners are square, that is, at right angles, and test this
with a tape or ruler by measuring six feet one way and
eight feet the other from a corner along the proposed sides
of the house marking these points. If a ten-foot rod will
reach exactly across from point to point, the corner is
square and you may dig your post-holes.

The Foundation

You may use a foundation of stones or a series of stone
piles, but if you use stones and expect your house to remain plumb where the winters are severe you must dig
holes for them at least three feet deep in order to go below
the frost-line. Fill these holes with broken stone, on top
of which you can make your pile of stones to act as support for the sills; but the simplest method is to use posts
of locust, cedar, or chestnut; or, if this is too much trouble,

39

pack the dirt tightly, drain it well by making it slope away
from the house in every direction, and lay your foundation
sills on the level earth.   In that case you had better use
chestnut wood for the sills; spruce will rot very quickly in
contact with the damp earth and pine will not last long
under the same circumstances.

All through certain sections of this country there are
hundreds of humble dwellings built upon "mudsills," in
other words, with no foundation or floor but the bare
ground.

We will suppose that you have secured some posts about
two feet six inches long with good, flat ends.   The better
material you can obtain the trimmer and better will be
the appearance of your house, but a house which will protect you and your tools may be made of the roughest
lumber.

The plans here drawn will answer for the rough or fine
material, but we suppose that medium material is to be
used.   It will be taken for granted that the reader is
able to procure enough two-by-four-inch timber to supply studs, ribs, purlins, rafters, beams, and posts for the
frame shown in Fig. 49.   Two pieces of four-by-four-inch
timber each fifteen feet long should be made for sills by
nailing two-by-fours together.   Add to this some tongue-
and-grooved boarding or even rough boards for sides and
roof, some enthusiasm, and good American pluck and the
shop is almost as good as built.

First lay the foundation, eight by fifteen feet, and then
you may proceed to dig your post-holes.   The outside of
the posts should be flush or even with the outside edges
of the sills and end beams of the house as shown in the
diagram.   If there are four posts on each of the long sides
they should be equal distances apart.

Dig the holes three feet deep, allowing six inches of the
posts to protrude above ground.   If you drive two stakes

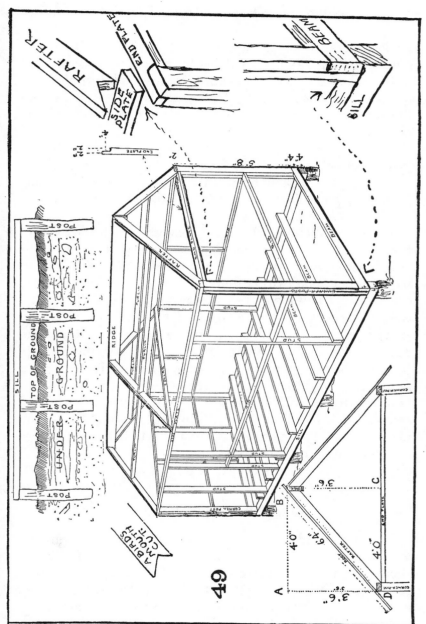

Frame of two-by-fours milled lumber, with names of parts.

a short distance beyond the foundation in line with your foundation lines and run a string from the top of one stake to the top of the other you can, without much trouble, get it upon a perfect level by testing it and adjusting until the string represents the level for your sill.   When this is done, set your posts to correspond to the level of the string, then place your sill on top of the posts and test that with your level.   If found to be correct, fill in the dirt around the posts and pack it firmly, then spike your sill to the posts and go through the same operation with opposite sets of posts and sill.

The first difficult work is now done and, with the exception of the roof, the rest only needs ordinary care.

It is supposed that you have already sawed off and prepared about nine two-by-four-inch beams each of which is exactly eight feet long.   Set these on edge from sill to sill, equal distances apart, the edges of the end beams being exactly even with the ends of the sills as in Fig. 49. See that the beams all cross the sills at right angles and toe-nail them in place.   You may now neatly floor the foundation with one-inch boards; these boards must be laid lengthwise with the building and crosswise with the beams.   When this is finished you will have a beautiful platform on which to work, where you will be in no danger of losing your tools, and you may use the floor as a table on which to measure and plan the sides and roof.

Ridge Plank and Rafters

It is a good idea to make your ridge plank and rafters while the floor is clear of rubbish.   Lay out and mark on the floor, with a carpenter's soft pencil, a straight line four feet long (*A*, *B*, Fig. 49).   At right angles to this draw another line three feet six inches long (*A*, *D*, Fig. 49). Connect these points (*B*, *D*, Fig. 49) with a straight line.

then complete the figure *A, B, C, D* (Fig. 49). Allow two inches at the top for the ridge plank at *B* and two by four for the end of the side-plate at *D*. You then have a pattern for each rafter with a "plumb edge" at *B* and a "bird's mouth" at *D*. The plumb edge must be parallel with *B, C* and the two jaws of the "bird's mouth" parallel with *D, C* and *A, D*, respectively. Make six rafters of two-by-fours and one ridge plank.

The purlins and collar can be made and fitted after the roof is raised. Set your roof timber carefully to one side and clear the floor for the studs, ribs, and plates. First prepare the end posts and make them of two-by-fours. Each post is of two pieces. There will be four outside pieces each five feet eight inches in length, which rest on the end beams, and four inside pieces each six feet in length; this allows two inches at the top for the ends of the end plates to rest upon.

Examine the corner posts and you will see that the outside two-by-four rests upon the top side of the end beam and the side-plate rests directly upon said two-by-four. You will also observe that the inside two-by-four rests directly upon the sill, which would make the former four inches longer than the outside piece if it is extended to the side-plate; but you will also notice that there is a notch in the end plate for the outside corner piece to fit in and that the end of the end plate fits on top the inside piece of the corner posts, taking off two inches, which makes the inside piece just six feet long. This is a very simple arrangement, as may be seen by examining the diagram. Besides the corner posts, each of which we have seen is made of two pieces of two-by-fours, there are four studs for the front side, each six feet two inches long. The short studs shown in the diagram on the rear side are unnecessary and are only shown so that they may be put in as convenient attachments for shelves and tool racks.

The first stud on the front is placed two feet from the corner post and the second one about six feet six inches from the first, to allow a space for a six-foot window; the next two studs form the door-jambs and must be far enough from the corner to allow the door to open and swing out of the way. If you make your door two and one half feet wide—a good size—you may set your last stud two feet from the corner post and leave a space of two feet six inches for the doorway. Now mark off on the floor the places where the studs will come, and cut out the flooring at these points to allow the ends of the studs to enter and rest on the sill. Next make four ribs—one long one to go beneath the window, one short one to fit between the corner post and the door stud not shown in diagram, another to fit between the door stud and window stud, and another to fit between the window stud and the first corner post (the nearest corner in the diagram). Next make your side-plate exactly fifteen feet long. Fit the frame together on the floor and nail the pieces together, toe-nailing the ribs in place. Get some help and raise the whole side frame and slip the ends of the studs into their respective slots. Make the end posts plumb and hold them in place temporarily by a board, one end of which is nailed to the top end of the post and the other to the end beam. Such a diagonal board at each end will hold the side in place until the opposite side is raised and similarly supported.

It is now a simple thing to slip the end plates in place under the side-plates until their outside edges are even with the outside of the corner posts. A long wire nail driven through the top-plates and end plates down into the posts at each corner will hold them securely. Toe-nail a rib between the two nearest end posts and make two window studs and three ribs for the opposite end. The framing now only needs the roof timbers to complete the skeleton of your shop. Across from side-plate to side-plate lay some loose boards for a platform, and standing on these boards let your assistant lift one end of the ridge plank while with one nail to each rafter you fasten the two end rafters onto the ridge plank, fit the jaws of the "bird's mouth" over the ends of the side-plates, and hold them temporarily in place with a "stay lath"—that is, a piece of board temporarily nailed to rafter and end plate. The other end of the ridge is now resting on the platform at the other end of the house and this may be lifted up, for the single nails will allow movement.

The rafters are nailed in place with one nail each and a stay lath fastened on to hold them in place. Test the ends with your plumb-level and when they are found to be correct nail all the rafters securely in place and stiffen the centre pair with a piece called a "collar." Add four purlins set at right angles to the rafters and take off your hat and give three cheers and do not forget to nail a green bough to your rooftree in accordance with the ancient and time-honored custom.

The sides of the house may be covered with tent-cloth, oilcloth, tin, tar paper, or the cheapest sort of lumber, and the house may be roofed with the same material; but if you can secure good lumber, use thirteen by seven eighths by nine and one quarter inch, tongue-and-grooved, one side planed so that it may be painted; you can make two sideboards out of each piece six feet six inches in length. Nail the sides on, running the boards vertically, leaving openings for windows and doors at the proper places.

If you have made a triangular edge to your ridge board, it will add to the finish and the roof may be neatly and tightly laid with the upper edge of one side protruding a couple of inches over the opposite side and thus protecting the joint from rain. Additional security is gained by nailing what are called picket strips (seven

eighths by one and three quarter inches) over each place
where the planks join, or the roof may be covered with
sheathing boards and shingles. It is not necessary here
to give the many details such as the manufacture of the
door and the arrangements of the windows, as these small
problems can be easily solved by examining doors and
windows of similar structures.

XI

A SOD HOUSE FOR THE LAWN

THE difference between this sod house and the ones used in the arid regions consists in the fact that the sod will be growing on the sod house, which is intended for and is an ornamental building for the lawn. Possibly one might say that the sod house is an effete product of civilization where utility is sacrificed to display; but it is pretty, and beauty is always worth while; besides which the same plans may be used in building

A Real Adobe

and practically are used in some of the desert ranches along the Colorado River. The principal difference in construction between the one shown in Figs. 50, 53, and 57 and the one in Fig. 55 is that in the sod house the sod is held in place by chicken-coop wire, while in the ranch-house (Fig. 55) the dirt or adobe is held in place by a number of sticks.

Fig. 50 shows how the double walls are made with a space of at least a foot between them; these walls are covered with wire netting or chicken-coop wire, as shown in Fig. 53, and the space between the walls filled in with mud or dirt of any kind. The framework may be made of milled lumber, as in Fig. 50, or it may be made of saplings cut on the river bank and squared at their ends, as shown by detailed drawings between Figs. 50 and 52. The roof may be made flat, like Figs. 54 and 56, and covered with

47

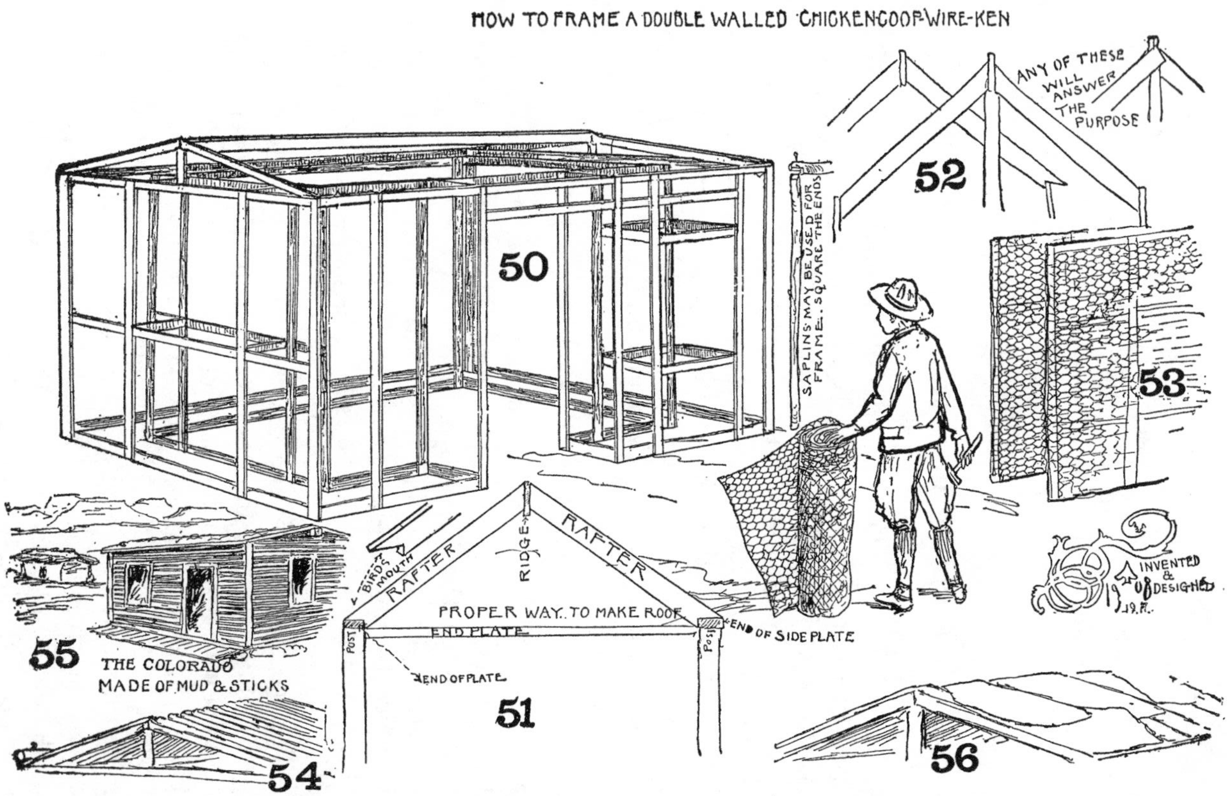

HOW TO FRAME A DOUBLE WALLED CHICKEN COOP WIRE-KEN

ANY OF THESE WILL ANSWER THE PURPOSE

52

53

50

SAPLINS MAY BE USED FOR FRAME. SQUARE THE ENDS

RAFTER

RIDGE

RAFTER

Bird's Mouth

PROPER WAY TO MAKE ROOF

End OF SIDE PLATE

END OF PLATE

POST

POST

51

55

THE COLORADO MADE OF MUD & STICKS

54

56

INVENTED & DESIGNED J.P.

A house of green growing sod and the Colorado River adobe.

poles, as in Fig. 54, in which case the sod will have to be held in place by pegging other poles along the eaves as shown in the left-hand corner of Fig. 54. This will keep the sod from sliding off the roof. Or you may build a roof after the manner illustrated by Fig. 49 and Fig. 51, that is, if you want to make a neat, workmanlike house; but any of the ways shown by Fig. 52 will answer for the framework of the roof. The steep roof, however, must necessarily be either shingled or thatched or the sod held in place by a covering of wire netting. If you are building this for your lawn, set green, growing sod up edgewise against the wire netting, after the latter has been tacked to your frame, so arranging the sod that the green grass will face the outside. If you wish to plaster the inside of your house with cement or concrete, fill in behind with mud, plaster the mud against the sod and put gravel and stones against the mud so that it will be next to the wire netting on the inside of the house over which you plaster the concrete. If you make the roof shown in Fig. 54, cover it first with hay and then dirt and sod and hold the sod down with wire netting neatly tacked over it, or cover it with gravel held in place by wire netting and spread concrete over the top as one does on a cellar floor. If the walls are kept sprinkled by the help of the garden hose, the grass will keep as green as that on your lawn, and if you have a dirt roof you may allow purple asters and goldenrod to grow upon it (Fig. 62) or plant it with garden flowers.

Thatch

If you are going to make a thatched roof, soak your thatch in water and straighten the bent straws; build the roof steep like the one shown in Fig. 57 and make a wooden needle a foot long and pointed at both ends as shown in

Fig. 59; tie your thatching twine to the middle of the needle, then take your rye or wheat straw, hay, or bulrushes, gather it into bundles four inches thick and one foot wide, like those shown in Fig. 60, and lay them along next to the eaves of your house as in Fig. 58. Sew them in place by running the needle up through the wire netting to the man on the outside who in turn pushes it back to the man on the inside. Make a knot at each wisp of the thatch until one layer is finished, let the lower ends overhang the eaves, then proceed as illustrated by Fig. 66 and described under the heading of the bog ken.

If in place of a simple ornament you want to make a real house of it and a pretty one at that, fill up the space between the walls with mud and plaster it on the outside with cement or concrete and you will have a cheap concrete house. The wire netting will hold the plaster or the concrete and consequently it is not necessary to make the covering of cement as thick as in ordinary buildings, for after the mud is dried upon the inside it will, with its crust of cement or plaster, be practically as good as a solid concrete wall.

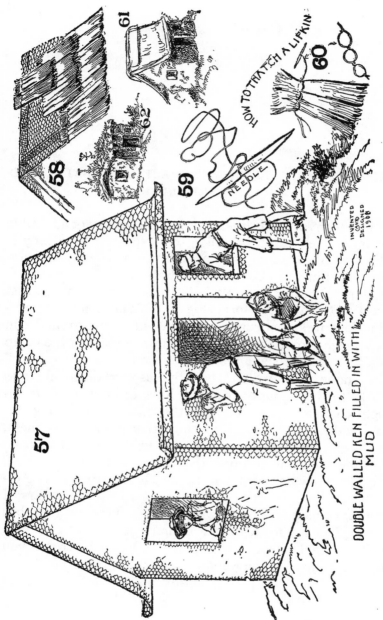

57

58

59

60

61

62

DOUBLE WALLED KEN FILLED IN WITH MUD

HOW TO THATCH A LIFKIN

NEEDLE

INVENTED AND DESIGNED 1900

Ornamental sod house for the lawn.

XII

HOW TO BUILD ELEVATED SHACKS, SHANTIES, AND SHELTERS

FOR many reasons it is sometimes necessary or advisable to have one's camp on stilts, so to speak. Especially is this true in the more tropical countries where noxious serpents and insects abound. A simple form of stilted shack is shown by Fig. 63. To build this shack we must first erect an elevated platform (Fig. 64). This is made by setting four forked sticks of equal height in the ground and any height from the ground to suit the ideas of the camp builder. If, for some reason, the uprights are "wabbly" the frame may be stiffened by lashing diagonal cross sticks to the frame. After you have erected the four uprights, lay two poles through the crotches, as in Fig. 64, and make a platform by placing other poles across these, after which a shelter may be made in the form of an open Adirondack camp or any of the forms previously described. Fig. 65 shows the framework for the open camp of Adirondack style with the uprights lashed to the side bars; if you have nails, of course, you can nail these together, but these plans are made on the assumption that you have no nails for that purpose, which will probably be true if you have been long in the woods.

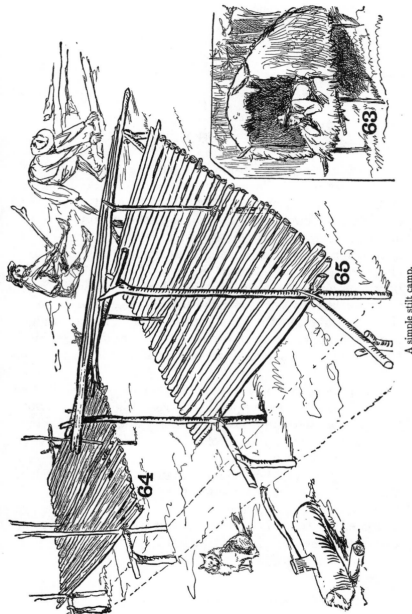

A simple stilt camp.

XIII

THE BOG KEN

Ken is a name now almost obsolete but the bog ken is a house built on stilts where the ground is marshy, damp, and unfit to sleep upon. As you will see by the diagram (Fig. 66), the house is built upon a platform similar to the one last described; in this instance, however, the shelter itself is formed by a series of arches similar to the Iroquois (Fig. 41). The uprights on the two sides have their ends bent over and lashed together, forming arches for the roof. Over the arches are lashed horizontal poles the same as those described in the construction of the Iroquois lodge. Fig. 67 shows one way to prevent "varmints" of any kind from scaling the supporting poles and creeping into your camp.

The protection consists of a tin pan with a hole in the bottom slid over the supporting poles. Fig. 66 shows how to lash the thatching on to the poles and Fig. 68 shows how to spring the sticks in place for a railing around your front porch or balcony.

The floor to this bog ken is a little more elaborate than that of the last described camp because the poles have all been halved before laying them for the floor. These are supposed to be afterward covered with browse, hay, or rushes and the roof shingled with bark or thatched.

Thatching

Soak your straw or hay well in water and smooth it out flat and regular. The steeper the roofs the longer

Details of bog ken.

the thatch will last. In this bog ken our roof happens to be a rounded one, an arched roof; but it is sheltering a temporary house and the thatch will last as long as the shack. While the real pioneer uses whatever material he finds at hand, it does no harm for him to know that to make a really good thatch one should use only straw which is fully ripe and has been thrashed clean with an old-fashioned flail. The straw must be clear of all seed or grain and kept straight, not mussed up, crumpled, and broken. If any grain is left in the straw it will attract field-mice, birds, domestic mice and rats, domestic turkeys and chickens, and these creatures in burrowing and scratching for food will play havoc with the roof.

It is not necessary to have straight and even rafters, because the humps, bumps, and hollows caused by crooked sticks are concealed by the mattress of straw. Take a bundle of thatch in your hands, squeeze it together, and place it so that the butt ends project about three inches beyond the floor (*A*, Fig. 66); tie the thatch closely to the lower rafter and the one next above it, using for the purpose twine, marlin, raffia, or well-twisted white hickory bark. This first row should be thus tied near both ends to prevent the wind from getting under it and lifting it up. Next put on another row of wisps of thatch over the first and the butt ends come even with the first, but tie this one to the third row of rafters not shown in diagram. The butts of the third row of thatch (*B*, Fig. 66) should be about nine inches up on the front rows; put this on as before and proceed the same way with *C*, *D*, *E*, and *F*, Fig. 66, until the roof is completed. The thatch should be ten or twelve inches thick for a permanent hut but need not be so for a temporary shed.

As there is no comb to this roof the top must be protected where the thatches from each side join, and to do this fasten a thatch over the top and bind it on both sides

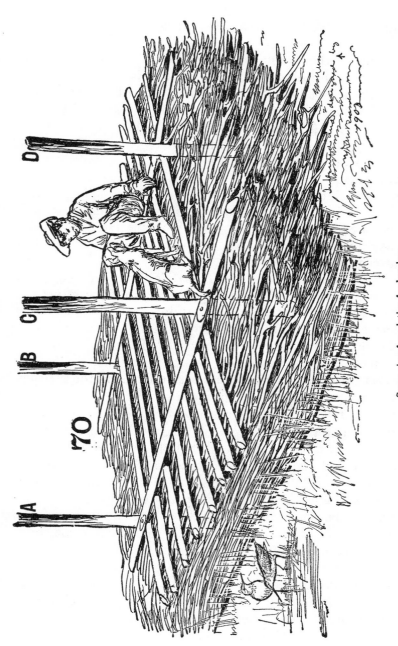

Snow-shoe foundation for bog ken.

but not in the middle, so that it covers the meeting of the thatches on both sides of the shack; this top piece should be stitched or bound on with wire if you have it, or fastened with willow withe or even wisps of straw if you are an expert.   A house, twenty by thirty feet, made of material found on the place and thatched with straw costs the builder only fifty cents for nails and four days' work for two persons.   A good thatched roof will last as long as a modern shingle roof, for in olden days when shingles were good and split out of blocks, not sawed, and were well seasoned before using, they were not expected to last much over fifteen years; a well-made thatched roof will last fifteen or twenty years.

But a real bog ken is one that is built over boggy or marshy places too soft to support an ordinary structure. To overcome this difficulty required considerable study and experiment, but at length the author hit upon a simple plan which has proved effective.   If you wish to build a duck hunter's camp on the soft meadows, or for any other reason you desire a camp on treacherous, boggy ground, you may build one by first making a thick mattress of twigs and sticks as shown by Fig. 70.   This mattress acts on the principle of a snow-shoe and prevents your house from sinking by distributing the weight equally over a wide surface.   The mattress should be carefully made of sticks having their branches trimmed off sufficiently to allow them to lie in regular courses as in the diagram.   The first course should be laid one way and the next course at right angles to the first, and so on, until the mattress is sufficiently thick for the purpose.

Standing on the mattress, it will be an easy matter with your hands to force the sharpened ends of your upright posts *A*, *B*, *C*, and *D* down into the yielding mud, but be careful not to push them too far because in some of these marshes the mud is practically bottomless.   It is only

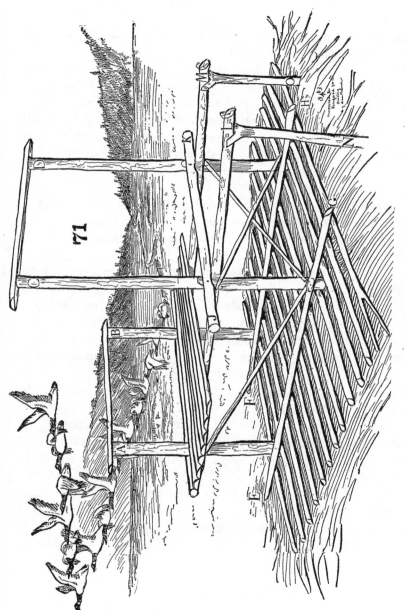

71

Framework of simple bog ken.

necessary for the supports to sink in the mud far enough to make them stand upright.

The next step is to lay, at right angles to the top layer of brush, a series of rods or poles between your uprights as shown in Fig. 70; then take two more poles, place them at right angles to the last ones, and press them down until they fit snugly on top of the other poles, and there nail them fast to the uprights as shown in Fig. 70, after which to further bind them you may nail a diagonal from A to D and B to C, but this may not be necessary.

When you have proceeded thus far you may erect a framework like that shown in Fig. 71, and build a platform by flooring the crosspieces or horizontal bars with halves of small logs, Fig. 71.

It is now a simple matter to erect a shack which may be roofed with bark as in Fig. 72 or thatched as in Fig. 74. Fig. 72 shows the unfinished shack in order that its construction may be easily seen; this one is being roofed with birch bark. A fireplace may be made by enclosing a bed of mud (Fig. 73) between or inside of the square formed by four logs. On this clay or mud you can build your camp-fire or cooking fire or mosquito smudge with little or no danger of setting fire to your house.

The mosquito smudge will not be found necessary if there is any breeze blowing at all, because these insects cling to the salt hay or bog-grass and do not rise above it except in close, muggy weather where no breeze disturbs them. I have slept a few feet over bog meadows without being disturbed by mosquitoes when every blade of grass on the meadows was black with these insects, but there was a breeze blowing which kept the mosquitoes at home.

THE BOG-KEN

72 A ADAPTATION OF A BARK SHACK TO A FOUNDATION INVENTED D. DESIGNED BY DAN BEARD 1903

73 CLAY OR MUD

MUD. Fire Place

DETAIL OF JOINT

74 A TINGUIANE BOG-KEN

Adaptation of a bark shack to the bog ken foundation.

XIV

OVER-WATER CAMPS

Now that we know how to camp on solid ground and on the quaking bog we cannot finish up the subject of stilt camps without including one over-water camp. If the water has a muddy bottom it is a simple matter to force your supporting posts into the mud; this may be done by driving them in with a wooden mallet made of a section of log or it may be done by fastening poles on each side of the post and having a crowd of men jump up and down on the poles until the posts are forced into the bottom.

If you are building a pretentious structure the piles may be driven with the ordinary pile-driver. But if your camp on the water is over a hard bottom of rock or sand through which you cannot force your supports you may take a lot of old barrels (Fig. 75), knock the tops and bottoms out of them, nail some cross planks on the ends of your spiles, slide the barrels over the spiles, then set them in place in the water and hold them there by filling the barrels with rocks, stones, or coarse gravel. Fig. 77 shows a foundation made in this manner; this method is also useful in building piers (Fig. 78). But if you are in the woods, out of reach of barrels or other civilized lumber, you can make yourself cribs by driving a square or a circle of sticks in the ground a short distance and then twining roots or pliable branches inside and outside the stakes, basket fashion, as shown in Fig. 76. When the crib is complete it may be carefully removed from the ground

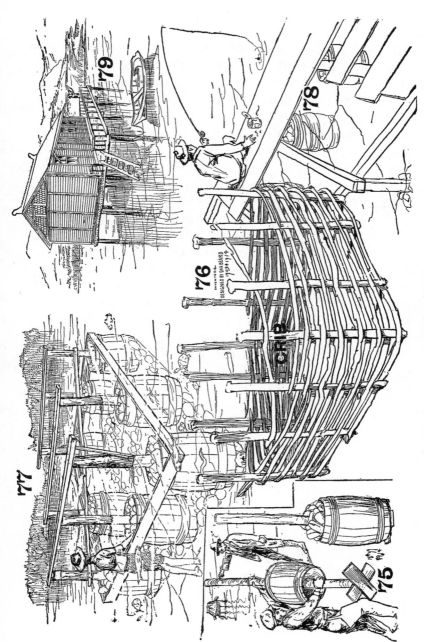

Showing how to make foundations for over water camps.

and used as the barrels were used by filling them with stones to support the uprights. Fig. 79 shows an ordinary portable house such as are advertised in all the sportsmen's papers, which has been erected upon a platform over the water.

My experience with this sort of work leads me to advise the use of piles upon which to build in place of piers of stones. Where I have used such piers upon small inland lakes the tremendous push of the freezing ice has upset them, whereas the ice seems to slide around the piles without pushing them over. The real danger with piles lies in the fact that if the water rises after the ice has frozen around the uprights the water will lift the ice up and the ice will sometimes pull the piles out of the bottom like a dentist pulls teeth. Nevertheless, piles are much better for a foundation for a camp or pier than any crib of rocks, and that is the reason I have shown the cribs in Figs. 75 and 77, made so as to rest upon the bottom supposedly below the level of the winter ice.

XV

SIGNAL-TOWER, GAME LOOKOUT, AND RUSTIC OBSERVATORY

I<small>F</small> my present reader happens to be a Boy Scout or a scout-master who wants the scouts to build a tower for exhibition purposes, he can do so by following the directions here given, but if there is real necessity for haste in the erection of this tower, of course we cannot build one as tall as we might where we have more time. With a small tower all the joints may be quickly lashed together with strong, heavy twine, rope, or even wire; and in the wilderness it will probably be necessary to bind the joints with pliable roots, or cordage made of bark or withes; but as this is not a book on woodcraft we will suppose that the reader has secured the proper material for fastening the joints of the frame of this signal-tower and he must now shoulder his axe and go to the woods in order to secure the necessary timber. First let him cut eight straight poles—that is, as straight as he can find them. These poles should be about four and one half inches in diameter at their base and sixteen and one half feet long. After all the branches are trimmed off the poles, cut four more sticks each nine feet long and two and a half or three inches in diameter at the base; when these are trimmed into shape one will need twenty six or seven more stout sticks each four and one half feet long for braces and for flooring for the platform.

Kite Frame

It being supposed that your timber is now all in readiness at the spot where you are to erect the tower, begin by laying out on the ground what we call the "kite frame." First take three of the four-and-one-half-foot sticks, A, B, C (Fig. 82), and two of the nine-foot sticks D and E (Fig. 82), and, placing them on a level stretch of ground, arrange them in the form of a parallelogram. Put A for the top rail at the top of the parallelogram and C for the bottom of the parallelogram and let them rest upon the sides D and E, but put B under the sides D and E. In order to bind these together securely, the ends of all the sticks must be allowed to project a few inches. B should be far enough below A to give the proper height for a railing around the platform. The platform itself rests upon B. A forms the top railing to the fence around it.

Now take two of your sixteen-and-one-half-foot poles and place them diagonally from corner to corner of the parallelogram with the small ends of the poles lying over the ends of A and the butt ends of the poles extending beyond C, as in Fig. 82. Lash these poles securely in place.

Where the poles cross each other in the X, or centre, it is best to flatten them some by scoring and hewing with a hatchet, but care must be taken not to weaken them by scoring too deep. Next take your lash rope, double it, run the loop down under the cross sticks, bring it up on the other side, as in Fig. 83, then pull the two loose ends through the loop. When they are drawn taut (Fig. 84), bend them round in opposite directions—that is, bend the right-hand end of the rope to the right, down and under the cross sticks, pull it out to the left, as in Fig. 84, then bend the left-hand piece of rope to the left, down and

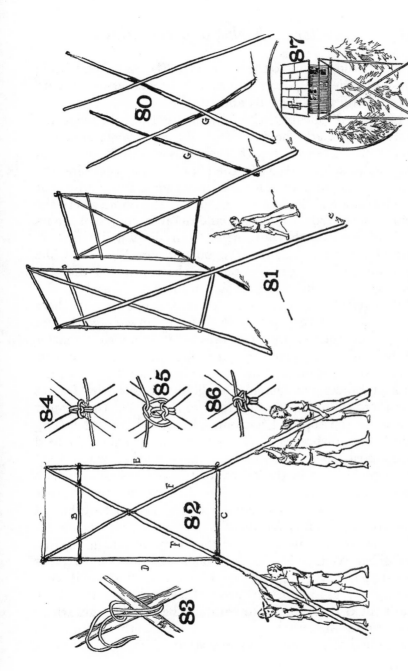

Parts of tower for a wireless, a game lookout, an elevated camp or cache.

under, pulling it out to the right, as in Fig. 84. Next bring
those two pieces up over and tie them together in a square
knot, as shown in Figs. 85 and 86.

Make a duplicate "kite" frame for the other side exactly as you made the first one, and then arrange these two
pieces on the ground with the cross sticks F and F on
the under-side and with their butt ends opposite the
butts of the similar poles on the other frame and about
five feet apart. Fasten a long line to the point where the
two F pieces cross each other and detail a couple of scouts
to hold each of the butt ends from slipping by placing
one of their feet against the butt, as in Fig. 82, while
two gangs of men or boys pull on the ropes and raise the
kite frames to the positions shown in Figs. 81 and 88.

Be careful, when raising the frames, not to pull them
too far so that they may fall on some unwary workman.
When the frames are once erected it is an easy matter
to hold them in place by guy-ropes fastened to stones,
stakes, or trees or held by men or boys, while some of the
shorter braces are fastened to hold the two kite frames
together, as in Fig. 90, wherein you may see these short
braces at the top and bottom. Next, the two other long
sticks, legs, or braces (G, G, Figs. 89 and 90) should be held
temporarily in position and the place marked where they
cross each other in the centre of the parallelogram which
should be the same as it is on the legs of the two kite
frames. The G sticks should now be lashed together at
the crossing point, as already described and shown by
Figs. 83, 84, 85, and 86, when they may be put up against
the sides, as in Fig. 89, in which diagram the G poles
are made very dark and the kite frames indicated very
lightly so as to better show their relative positions.
Lash the G poles at the top and at the other points where
they cross the other braces and secure the framework
by adding short braces, as indicated in Fig. 90.

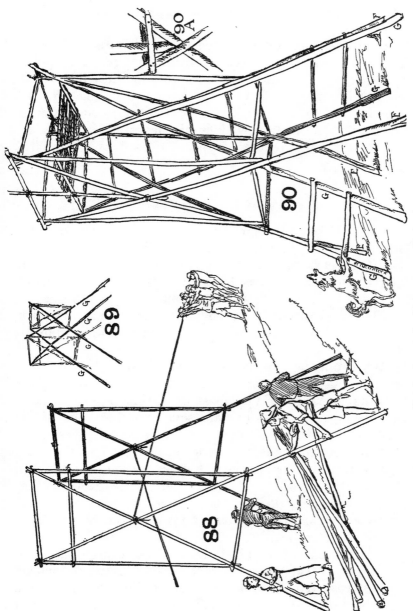

Details of scout signal-tower or game lookout.

If all the parts are bound together with wire it will hold them more securely than nails, with no danger of the poles splitting. A permanent tower of this kind may be erected on which a camp may be built, as shown in Fig. 87. It may be well to note that in the last diagram the tower is only indicated by a few lines of the frame in order to simplify it and prevent confusion caused by the multiplicity of poles.

Boy-Scout Tower

If you desire to make a tower taller than the one described it would be best, perhaps, to take the regular Boy-Scout dimensions as given by Scout-master A. G. Clarke:

"Eight pieces 22 feet long, about 5 or 6 inches thick at the base; 4 pieces 6 feet long, about 3 or 4 inches thick at the base; 12 pieces 6 feet long, about 2½ or 3 inches thick at base; 12 or 15 pieces for braces and platform about 6 feet long."

When putting together this frame it may be nailed or spiked, but care must be used not to split the timber where it is nailed. With most wood this may be avoided by driving the spikes or nails several inches back of the ends of the sticks. To erect a flagpole or a wireless pole, cut the bottom of the pole wedge-shaped, fit it in the space between the cross poles, as in Fig. 90 *A*, then lash it fast to the *B* and *A* pole, and, to further secure it, two other sticks may be nailed to the *F* poles, one on each side, between which the bottom of the flagpole is thrust, as shown by Fig. 90 *A*.

The flooring of the platform must be securely nailed or lashed in place, otherwise there may be some serious accident caused by the boys or men falling through, a fall of about twenty and one half feet according to the last measurements given for the frame.

An observatory of this kind will add greatly to the interest of a mountain home or seaside home; it is a practical tower for military men to be used in flag signalling and for improvised wireless; it is also a practical tower for a lookout in the game fields and a delight to the Boy Scouts.

XVI

TREE-TOP HOUSES

By the natural process of evolution we have now arrived at the tree-top house. It is interesting to the writer to see the popularity of this style of an outdoor building, for, while he cannot lay claim to originating it, he was the first to publish the working drawings of a tree-house. These plans first appeared in *Harper's Round Table;* afterward he made others for the *Ladies' Home Journal* and later published them in "The Jack of All Trades."

Having occasion to travel across the continent shortly after the first plans were published, he was amused to see all along the route, here and there in back-yard fruit-trees, shade-trees, and in forest-trees, queer little shanties built by the boys, high up among the boughs.

In order to build a house one must make one's plans *to fit the tree.* If it is to be a one-tree house, spike on the trunk two quartered pieces of small log one on each side of the trunk (Figs. 91 and 92). Across these lay a couple of poles and nail them to the trunk of the tree (Fig. 91); then at right angles to these lay another pair of poles, as shown in the right-hand diagram (Fig. 91). Nail these securely in place and support the ends of the four poles by braces nailed to the trunk of the tree below. The four cross-sills will then (Fig. 95) serve as a foundation upon which to begin your work. Other joists can now be laid across these first and supported by braces running diagonally down to the trunk of the tree, as shown in

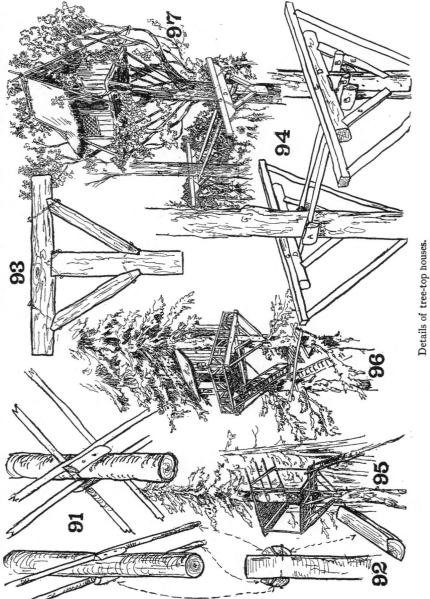

Details of tree-top houses.

Fig. 95. After the floor is laid over the joist any form of shack, from a rude, open shed to a picturesque thatch-roofed cottage, may be erected upon it. It is well to support the two middle rafters of your roof by quartered pieces of logs, as the middle rafters are supported in Fig. 95; by quartered logs shown in Fig. 92.

If the house is a two-tree house, run your cross-sill sticks from trunk to trunk, as in Fig. 94; then make two T-braces, like the one in Fig. 94 *A*, of two-inch planks with braces secured by iron straps, or use heavier timber, and bolt the parts together securely (Fig. 93), or use logs and poles (Fig. 94), after which hang these T's over the ends of your two cross sticks, as in Fig. 94, and spike the uprights of the T's securely to the tree trunks. On top of the T you can rest a two-by-four and support the end by diagonals nailed to the tree trunk (Fig. 94) after the manner of the diagonals in Fig. 95. You will note in Fig. 95 that cleats or blocks are spiked to the tree below the end of the diagonals in order to further secure them. It is sometimes necessary in a two-tree house to allow for the movement of the tree trunks. In Florida a gentleman did this by building his tree-house on the *B* sills (Fig. 94) and making them movable to allow for the play of the tree trunks. Fig. 96 shows a two-tree house and Fig. 97 shows a thatch-roofed cottage built among the top branches of a single tree.

It goes without saying that in a high wind one does not want to stay long in a tree-top house; in fact, during some winds that I have experienced I would have felt much safer had I been in a cyclone cellar; but if the braces of a tree-house are securely made and the trees selected have good, heavy trunks, your tree-top house will stand all the ordinary summer blows and winter storms. One must remember that even one's own home is not secure enough to stand some of those extraordinary gales, tornadoes, and hurricanes which occasionally visit parts of our country.

Since I published the first plans of a tree-top house many people have adopted the idea and built quite expensive structures in the boughs of the trees. Probably all these buildings are intact at the present writing.

The boys at Lynn, Mass., built a very substantial house in the trees, and the truant officer claimed that the lads hid away there so that they could play "hookey" from school; but if this is true, and there seems to be some doubt about it, it must be remembered that the fault was probably with *the schools* and not the boys, for boys who have ingenuity and grit enough to build a substantial house in a tree cannot be bad boys; industry, skill, and laborious work are not the attributes of the bad boy.

Some New York City boys built a house in the trees at One Hundred and Sixty-ninth Street, but here the police interfered, claiming that it was against a city ordinance to build houses in shade-trees, and maybe it is; but, fortunately for the boys, there are other trees which may be used for this purpose. There is now, or was recently, an interesting tree-house on Flatbush Avenue, Brooklyn; a house so commodious that it was capable of accommodating as many as fifteen people; but it was not as pretty and attractive a tree-house as the one located at the foot of Mount Tamalpais, in Mill Valley, San Francisco, which is built after the plan shown by Fig. 95. This California house is attached to the trunk of a big redwood tree and is reached by a picturesque bridge spanning a rocky canyon.

Tree-houses are also used as health resorts, and recently there was a gentleman of Plainfield, Mass., living in a tree-house because he found the pure air among the leaves beneficial; while down in Ecuador another man, who feared malarial mosquitoes and objected to wild beasts and snakes, built himself a house on top of an ibo-tree, seventy feet from the ground. This is quite a pretentious structure and completely hides and covers the top of the tree.   It is located on the banks of the Escondido River; and in this tropical country, while it may be a safe retreat from the pests enumerated, it might not be so safe from lightning in one of those violent tropical storms. But it is probably as safe as any house in that country, for one must take chances no matter what kind of a house one dwells in.

Primitive and savage men all over the world for thousands of years have built dwellings in tree tops.   In the Philippines many natives live in tree-top houses. The Kinnikars, hill-tribesmen of Travancore, India, are said to live in houses built in the trees, but in New Guinea it seems that such houses are only provided for the girls, and every night the dusky lassies are sent to bed in shacks perched in the tree tops; then, to make safety doubly safe, the watchful parents take away the ladders and their daughters cannot reach the ground until the ladders are replaced in the morning.

The most important thing about all this is that a tree-house is always a source of delight to the boys and young people, and, furthermore, the boys have over and over again proved to the satisfaction of the author that they themselves are perfectly competent to build these shacks, and not only to build them but to avoid accidents and serious falls while engaged in the work.

XVII

CACHES

THE difference between tomahawk shacks and axe houses reminds me of the difference between the ileum and the jejunum, of which my classmate once said: "There is no way of telling the beginning of one or the ending of t'other 'cept by the pale-pinkish hue of the latter."

It must be confessed that some of the shacks described in the preceding pages are rather stout and massive to be classed as tomahawk shelters, but, as indicated by my reference to physiology, this is not the writer's fault. The trouble is owing to the fact that nature abhors the arbitrary division line which man loves to make for his own convenience. The tomahawk shacks gradually evolve into axe camps and houses and "there is no telling the beginning of one and the end of t'other." Hence, when I say that all the previous shacks, sheds, shelters, and shanties are fashioned with a hatchet, the statement must be accepted as true only so far as *it is* possible to build them without an axe; but in looking over the diagram it is evident at a glance that the logs are growing so thick that the necessity of the woodman's axe is more and more apparent; nevertheless, the accompanying caches have been classed with the tomahawk group and we will allow them to remain there.

Wherever man travels in the wilderness he finds it neces-

Simple forms of caches.

sary to cache—that is, hide or secure some of his goods or provisions. The security of these caches (Figs. 98–111) is considered sacred in the wilds and they are not disturbed by savages or whites; but bears, foxes, husky dogs, porcupines, and wolverenes are devoid of any conscientious scruples and unless the cache is absolutely secure they will raid it.

The first cache (Fig. 98) is called the "prospector's cache" and consists simply of a stick lashed to two trees and another long pole laid across this to which the goods are hung, swinging beneath like a hammock. This cache is hung high enough to be out of reach of a standing bear.

The tripod cache (Fig. 100) consists of three poles lashed at the top with the goods hung underneath.

Another form of the prospector's cache is shown by Fig. 102, where two poles are used in place of one and an open platform of sticks laid across the poles; the goods are placed upon the platform.

The tenderfoot's cache (Fig. 105) is one used only for temporary purposes as it is too easily knocked over and would be of no use where animals as large as bears might wreck it. It consists of two sticks lashed together at their small ends and with their butt ends buried in the earth; their tops are secured by a rope to a near-by tree while the duffel is suspended from the top of the longest pole.

The "Montainais" cache is an elevated platform upon which the goods are placed and covered with skins or tarpaulin or tent-cloth (Fig. 99).

The "Andrew Stone" cache is a miniature log cabin placed on the ground and the top covered with halved logs usually weighted down with stones (Fig. 101).

The "Belmore Browne" cache consists of a pole or a half of a log placed in the fork of the two trees on top of which the goods are held in place by a rope and the whole covered with a piece of canvas lashed together with eye-lets, like a shoe (Fig. 103).

The "Herschel Parker" cache is used where the articles to be cached are in a box. For this cache two poles are lashed to two trees, one on each side of the trees (Fig. 104), and across the two poles the box is placed.

We now come to more pretentious caches, the first of which is the "Susitna," which is a little log cabin built on a table with four long legs. The poles or logs composing the legs of the table are cut in a peculiar fashion, as shown in the diagram to the left of Fig. 107; this is intended to prevent animals from climbing to the top; also, as a further protection, pieces of tin are sometimes tacked around the poles so as to give no foothold to the claws of the little animals.

Fig. 106 shows two other methods sometimes adopted to protect small caches and Fig. 108 is still another method of using logs which have the roots still attached to them for supports. Such logs can be used where the ground is too stony to dig holes for posts.

Fig. 109 shows another form of the Susitna cache wherein the goods are packed in a box-like structure and covered with tent-cloth tightly lashed down.

The "Dillon Wallace" cache (Fig. 110) is simply a tent erected over the goods and perched on an elevated plat-form.

The "Fred Vreeland" cache is a good, solid, practical storehouse. It is built of small logs on a platform, as shown by Fig. 111, and the bottom of the building is smaller than it is at the eaves. It is covered with a high thatched roof and is ornamental as well as useful.

These caches might really belong to a book of woodcraft, but it is another case of the "ileum and jejunum," and we will rule that they technically come under the head of shacks, sheds, shelters, and shanties and so are included

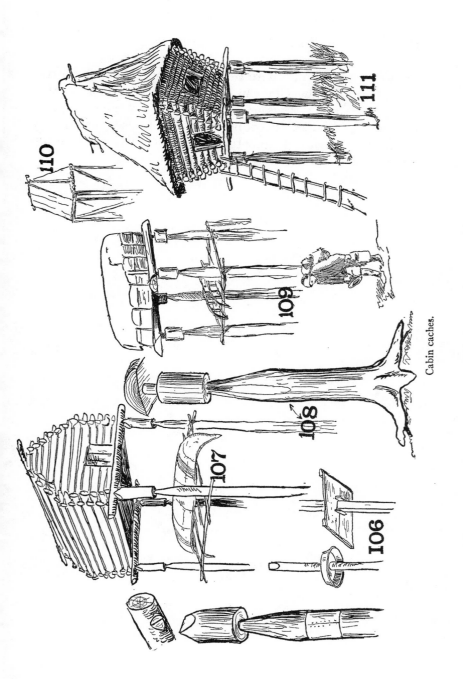

Cabin caches.

in this volume; but there is another and a very good reason for publishing them in this book, and that is because some of them, like Figs. 107 and 111, suggest novel forms of ornamental houses on country estates, houses which may be used for corn-cribs or other storage or, like the tree-top houses, used for pleasure and amusement.

XVIII

HOW TO USE AN AXE

THE old backwoodsmen were as expert with their axes as they were with their rifles and they were just as careful in the selection of these tools as they were in the selection of their arms. Many a time I have seen them pick up a "store" axe, sight along the handle, and then cast it contemptuously aside; they demanded of their axes that the cutting edge should be exactly in line with the point in the centre of the butt end of the handle. They also kept their axes so sharp that they could whittle with them like one can with a good jack-knife; furthermore, they allowed *no one* but themselves to use their own particular axe. In my log house in the mountains of Pike County, Pa., I have a table fashioned entirely with an axe; even the ends of the boards which form the top of the table were cut off by Siley Rosencranz with his trusty axe because he had no saw.

Both General Grant and Abraham Lincoln were expert axemen, and probably a number of other Presidents were also skilful in the use of this tool; but it is not expected that the modern vacation pioneer shall be an expert, consequently a few simple rules and suggestions will be here given to guide the amateur and he must depend upon his own judgment and common sense to work out the minor problems which will beset him in the use of this tool.

Dangers

All edged tools are dangerous when in the hands of "chumps," dangerous to themselves and to any one else who is near them. For instance, only a chump will use an axe when its head is loose and is in danger of flying off the handle; only a chump will use his *best* axe to cut roots or sticks lying flat on the ground where he is liable to strike stones and other objects and take the edge off the blade. Only a chump will leave an axe lying around on the ground for people to stumble over; if there is a stump handy at your camp and you are through using the axe, strike the blade into the top of the stump and leave the axe sticking there, where it will be safe from injury.

Remember, before chopping down a tree or before using the axe at all, to see that there is enough space above and around you to enable you to swing the axe clear (Fig. 112) without the danger of striking bushes or overhanging branches which may deflect the blade and cause accidents more or less serious.

Do not stand behind a tree as it falls (Fig. 115), for the boughs may strike those of a standing tree, causing the butt to shoot back or "kick," and many a woodsman has lost his life from the kick of a falling tree. Before chopping a tree down, select the place where it is to fall, a place where it will not be liable to lodge in another tree on its way down. Do not try to fell a tree against the wind.

Cut a notch on the side of the tree facing the direction you wish it to fall (Fig. 113) and cut it half-way through the trunk. Make the notch, or kerf, large enough to avoid pinching your axe in it. If you discover that the notch is going to be too small, cut a new notch, *X* (Fig. 116), some inches above your first one, then split off the piece *X*, *Y* between the two notches, and again make

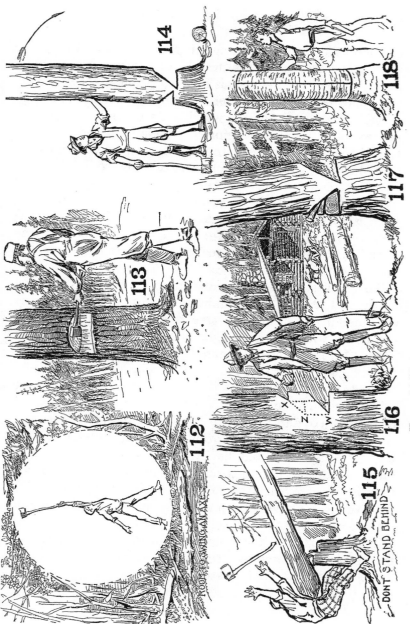

How to "fall" a tree and how to take off the bark.

the notch X, Z, and split off the piece Z, W, Y (Fig. 116), until you make room for the axe to continue your chopping. When the first kerf is finished begin another one on the opposite side of the tree a little higher than the first one (Fig. 114). When the wood between the two notches becomes too small to support the weight of the tree, the top of the tree will begin to tremble and waver and give you plenty of time to step to one side before it falls.

If the tree (Fig. 117) is inclined in the opposite direction from which you wish it to fall, it is sometimes possible (Fig. 117) to block up the kerf on the inclined side and then by driving the wedge over the block force the tree to fall in the direction desired; but if the tree inclines too far this cannot be done.

There was a chestnut-tree standing close to my log house and leaning toward the building. Under ordinary circumstances felling this tree would cause it to strike the house with all the weight of its trunk and branches. When I told Siley Rosencranz I wanted that tree cut down he sighted up the tree, took a chew of tobacco, and walked away. For several days he went through the same performance, until at last one day he brought out his trusty axe and made the chips fly. Soon the chestnut was lying prone on the ground *pointing away* from the house. What this old backwoodsman did was to wait until a strong wind had sprung up, blowing in the direction that he wanted the tree to fall, and his skilful chopping with the aid of the wind placed the tree exactly where he wished it.

Fig. 118 shows how to make the cuts on a standing tree in order to remove the bark, which is done in the same manner as that described for removing the birch bark (Fig. 38).

XIX

HOW TO SPLIT LOGS, MAKE SHAKES, SPLITS, OR CLAPBOARDS. HOW TO CHOP A LOG IN HALF. HOW TO FLATTEN A LOG. ALSO SOME DON'TS

Logs are usually split by the use of wedges, but it is possible to split them by the use of two axes. Fig. 119 shows both methods. To split with the axe, strike it smartly into the wood at the small end so as to start a crack, then sink the axe in the crack, *A*. Next take the second axe and strike it in line with the first one at *B*. If this is done properly it should open the crack wide enough to release the first axe without trouble, which may then be struck in the log at *C*. In this manner it is possible to split a straight-grained piece of timber without the use of wedges. The first axe should be struck in at the smaller or top end of the log. To split a log with wedges, take your axe in your left hand and a club in your right hand and, by hammering the head of your axe with the club, drive the blade into the small end of the log far enough to make a crack deep enough to hold the thin edge of your wedges. Make this crack all the way across the end of the log, as in Fig. 119. Put two wedges in the end of the log, as in the diagram, and drive them until the wood begins to split and crack along the sides of the log; then follow up this crack with other wedges, as shown at *D* and *E*, until the log is split in half.

While ordinary wood splits easily enough with the grain, it is very difficult to drive an axe through the wood

87

at right angles to the grain, as shown by diagram to the left (Fig. 120); hence, if the amateur be chopping wood, if he will strike a slanting blow, like the one to the right in Fig. 120, he will discover that the blade of his axe will enter the wood; whereas, in the first position, where he strikes the grain at right angles, it will only make a dent in the wood and bounce the axe back; but in striking a diagonal blow he must use care not to slant his axe too far or the blade of the axe may only scoop out a shallow chip and swing around, seriously injuring the axeman or some one else.

If it is desired to cut off the limb of a tree, do not disfigure the tree by tearing the bark down; trees are becoming too scarce for us to injure them unnecessarily; if you cut part way through the limb on the under-side (see the right-hand diagram, Fig. 121) and then cut partly through from the top side, the limb will fall off without tearing the bark down the trunk; but if you cut only from the top (see left-hand diagram, Fig. 121), sooner or later the weight of the limb will tear it off and make an ugly wound down the front of the tree, which in time decays, makes a hollow, and ultimately destroys the tree. A neatly cut branch, on the other hand, when the stub has been sheared off close to the bark, will heal up, leaving only an eye-mark on the bark to tell where the limb once grew.

If it is desired to chop a log up into shorter pieces, remember to stand on the log to do your chopping, as in Fig. 122. This will do away with the necessity of rolling the log over when you want to chop on the other side. Do not forget to make the kerf, or notch, C, D the same as A, B; in other words, the distance across the notch should equal the diameter of the log. If you start with too narrow a kerf, or notch, before you finish you will be compelled to widen it.

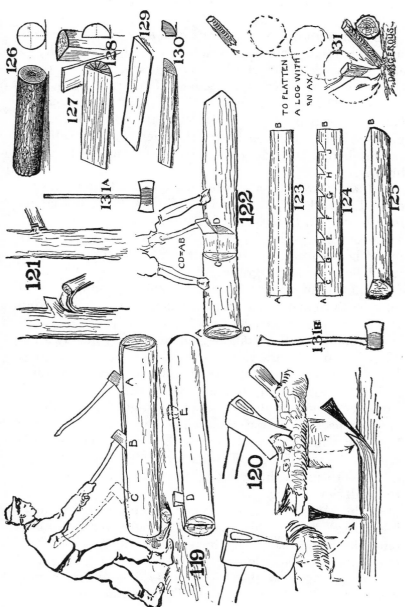

How to split a log, chop a log, flatten a log, and trim a tree.

To flatten a log you must *score and hew* it.   Scoring consists in making a number of notches, *C, D, E, F, G, H, J,*
etc., to the depth of the line *A, B* (Figs. 123 and 124);
hewing it is the act of chopping off or splitting off the
pieces *A, C* and *C, D* and *D, E,* etc., leaving the surface
flat, as shown by Fig. 125, which was known among the
pioneers as a puncheon and with which they floored their
cabins before the advent of the saw-mill and milled
lumber.

Perhaps it will be advisable for the amateur to take a
chalk-line and snap it from *A* to *B* (Fig. 123), so that he
may be certain to have the flat surface level.   The expert
axeman will do this by what he calls "sensiation."   It
might be well to say here that if you select for puncheons
wood with a straight grain and wood that will split easily
you will simplify your task, but even mean, stubborn wood
may be flattened by scoring and hewing.   Quoting from
Horace Kephart's excellent book on woodcraft, an experienced man can tell a straight-grained log "by merely scan-
ning the bark"; if the ridges and furrows of the bark run
straight up and down the wood will have a corresponding
straight grain, but if they are spiral the wood will split
"waney" or not at all.   "Waney" is a good word, almost
as good as "sensiation"; so when you try to quarter a
log with which to chink your cabin or log house don't
select a "waney" log.   To quarter a log split it as shown
in Fig. 119 and split it along the dotted lines shown in
the end view of Fig. 126.

In the Maine woods the woodsmen are adepts in making shakes, splits, clapboards, or shingles by the use of
only an axe and splitting them out of the billets of wood
from four to six feet long.   The core of the log (Fig. 130)
is first cut out and then the pieces are split out, having
wedge-shaped edges, as shown by the lines marked on
Fig. 127.   They also split out boards after the manner

shown by Fig. 128. In making either the boards or the shakes, if it is found that the wood splinters down into the body of the log too far or into the board or shake too far, you must commence at the other end of the billet or log and split it up to meet the first split, or take hold of the split or board with your hands and deftly tear it from the log, an art which only experience can teach. I have seen two-story houses composed of nothing but a framework with sides and roof shingled over with these splits. In the West they call these "shake" cabins.

It may be wise before we close this axeman's talk to caution the reader against chopping firewood by resting one end of the stick to be cut on a log and the other end on the ground, as shown in Fig. 131, and then striking this stick a sharp blow with the axe in the middle. The effect of this often is to send the broken piece or fragment gyrating through the air, as is shown by the dotted lines, and many a woodchopper has lost an eye from a blow inflicted by one of these flying pieces; indeed, I have had some of my friends meet with this serious and painful accident from the same cause, and I have seen men in the lumber fields who have been blinded in a similar manner.

There are two sorts of axes in general use among the lumbermen; but the double-bitted axe (131 *A*) appears to be the most popular among lumberjacks. My readers, however, are not lumberjacks but campers, and a double-bitted axe is a nuisance around camps. It is always dangerous and even when one blade is sunk into the tree the other blade is sticking out, a menace to everybody and everything that comes near it. But the real old-fashioned reliable axe (131 *B*) is the one that is exceedingly useful in a camp, around a country place, or a farm. I even have one now in my studio closet here in the city of New York, but I keep it more for sentiment's sake than for any real use it may be to me here.

XX

AXEMEN'S CAMPS

The Stefansson Sod Shack

Now that we know how to wield the axe we can begin on more ambitious structures than those preceding. We may now build camps in which we use logs instead of poles. Most of these camps are intended to be covered with sod or earth and are nearly related to the old prairie dugout. The sod house is used in the arctic regions because it is warm inside, and it is used in the arid regions because it is cool inside. You will note that the principle on which the Stefansson is constructed (Fig. 135) is practically the same as that of the Pontiac (Fig. 36); the Stefansson frame, however, is made of larger timbers than the Pontiac because it not only must support a roof and side of logs and sod but must also be able to sustain any quantity of snow.

First erect two forked upright sticks (Fig. 132), and then steady them by two braces. Next lay four more logs or sticks for the side-plates with their butt ends on the ridge-pole and their small ends on the ground as in Fig. 133. Support these logs by a number of small uprights—as many as may be necessary for the purpose. The uprights may have forks at the top or have the top ends cut wedge-shaped to fit in notches made for that purpose in the side-plates as shown by Fig. 133 *A*. The shortest uprights at the end of the roof should be forked so that

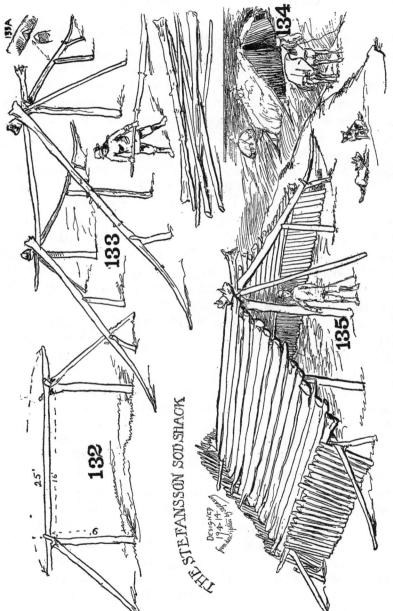

THE STEFANSSON SOD SHACK

Designed
1914
from description by Stefansson

Details of the Stefansson sod shack.

the projecting fork will tend to keep the roof logs from sliding down. The roof is made by a number of straight rafters placed one with the butt in front, next with the butt in the rear alternately, so that they will fit snugly together until the whole roof is covered. The sides are made by setting a number of sticks in a trench and slanting them against the roof; both sides, front, and rear of the building should project six inches above the roof in order to hold the sod and dirt and keep it from sliding off.

Up in the north country one must not expect to find green, closely cropped lawns or even green fields of wild sod in all places. Although in some parts the grass grows taller than a man's head, in other places the sod is only called so by courtesy; it really consists of scraggy grass thinly distributed on gravelly and sandy, loose soil, and consequently we must secure the sod by having the walls project a little above the rafters all around the building. Of course, in summer weather this roof will leak, but then one may live in a tent; but when cold weather comes and the sod is frozen hard and banked up with snow the Stefansson makes a good, warm dwelling.

The same style of a camp can be made in the temperate zone of smaller trees and shingled with browse, or in the South of cane or bamboo and shingled with palmetto leaves, or in the Southwest of cottonwood where it may be covered with adobe or mud. Fig. 134 shows a Stefansson shack roofed with sod. The front is left uncovered to show its construction and also to show how the doorway is made by simply leaving an opening like that in a tent. In winter this may have a hallway built like the one described in the Navajo earth lodge (Fig. 35) or in the Pawnee hogan (Figs. 42 and 43), and in milder weather the doorway may be protected with a skin. An opening is left in the roof over the fireplace, which answers the purpose of a chimney.

The author aims to take hints from all the primitive dwellings which may be of service to outdoor people; the last one described was arbitrarily named the Stefansson because that explorer built himself such shelters in the far North, but he did not invent them. He borrowed the general plan from the natives of the northern country and adapted it to his use, thereby placing the official stamp on this shack as a useful building for outdoor people and, consequently, as deserving a place in this book.

XXI

RAILROAD-TIE SHACKS, BARREL SHACKS, AND CHIMEHUEVIS

No observing person has travelled far upon the Ameri‹ can railroads without noticing, alongside the tracks, the queer little houses built of railroad ties by Italian laborers. These shacks are known by the name of dagoes (Fig. 136) and are made in different forms, according to the ingenuity of the builder. The simplest form is the tent-shaped shown in Fig. 136, with the ends of the ties rested together in the form of a tent and with no other support but their own weight (see the diagram to the right, Fig. 136). I would not advise boys to build this style, because it might make a trap to fall in upon them with serious results, but if they use a ridge-pole like the one shown in Fig. 139 and against it rest the ties they will do away with the danger of being caught in a deadfall trap. Of course, it is understood that the ridge-pole itself must first be secure.

Railroad ties being flat (Fig. 137), they may be built up into solid walls (Fig. 137) and make neat sides for a little house; or they may be set up on edge (Fig. 138) and secured in place by stakes driven upon each side of them; or they may be made into the form of an open Adirondack camp (Figs. 139 and 140) by resting the ties on a ridge-pole supported by a pair of "shears" at each end;

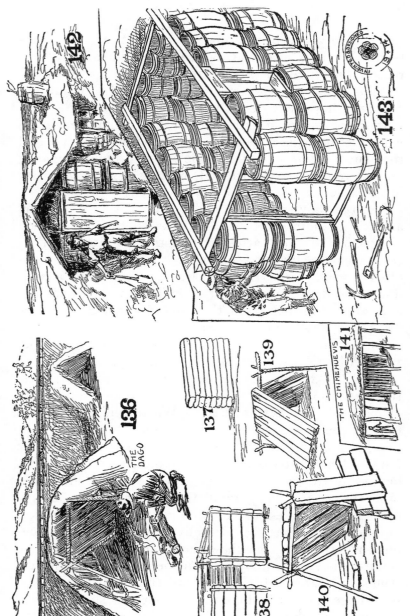

Railroad-tie shacks, barrel shack, and a Chimehuevis.

the shears, as you will observe, consist of two sticks bound together near the top and then spread apart to receive the ridge-pole in the crotch.

All of these structures are usually covered with dirt and sod, and they make very comfortable little camps.

In the Southwest a simple shelter, the "Chimehuevis," is made by enclosing a room in upright poles (Fig. 141) and then surrounding it with a circle of poles supporting a log or pole roof covered with sod, making a good camp for hot weather.

Fig. 142 shows a barrel dugout. It is made by digging a place for it in the bank and, after the floor is levelled off, setting rows of barrels around the foundation, filling these barrels with sand, gravel, or dirt, then placing another row on top of the first, leaving spaces for a window and a door, after which the walls are roofed with logs and covered with sod, in the same manner as the ones previously described. The dirt is next filled around the sides, except at the window opening, as shown by Fig. 142. A barrel also does duty as a chimney.

Shacks like this are used by homesteaders, miners, trappers, and hunters; in fact, these people use any sort of material they have at hand. When a mining-camp is near by the freight wagons are constantly bringing in supplies, and these supplies are done up in packages of some kind. Boards are frequently worth more a yard than silk, or were in the olden days, and so the home builders used other material. They built themselves houses of discarded beer bottles, of kerosene cans, of packing-boxes, of any and every thing. Usually these houses were dugouts, as is the barrel one shown in Fig. 142. In the big-tree country they not infrequently made a house of a hollow stump of a large redwood, and one stone-mason hollowed out a huge bowlder for his dwelling; but such shacks belong among the freak shelters. The barrel one, however, being the more practical and one that can be used almost any-where where timber is scarce but where goods are trans-ported in barrels, deserves a place here among our shacks, shelters, and shanties.

XXII

THE BARABARA

The houses along the coast of the Bering Sea are called barabaras, but the ones that we are going to build now are in form almost identical with the Pawnee hogan (Figs. 42 and 43), the real difference being in the peculiar log work of the barabara in place of the teepee-like rafters of the said hogan.

To build a barabara you will need eight short posts for the outside wall and six or eight longer posts for the inside supports (Fig. 145). The outside posts should stand about three feet above the ground after they have been planted in the holes dug for the purpose. The top of the posts should be cut wedge-shaped, as shown by Fig. 144, in order to fit in the notch B (Fig. 144). The cross logs, where they cross each other, should be notched like those of a log cabin (Figs. 162 and 165) or flattened at the points of contact.

Plant your first four posts for the front of your barabara in a line, two posts for the corners B and E (Fig. 145 A), and two at the middle of the line C and D for door-jambs (plan, Fig. 145 A). The tops of these posts should be level with each other so that if a straight log is placed over them the log will lie level. Next plant the two side-posts F and G (Fig. 145 A) at equal distances from the two front posts and make them a few feet farther apart than are the front posts. The sketch of the framework is drawn in very steep perspective, that is, it is made

The details of a Barabara.

as if the spectator was on a hill looking down upon it.   It is drawn in this manner so as to better show the construction, but the location of the posts may be seen in the small plan.   Next set the two back posts, *H* and *K*, and place them much closer together, so that the bottom frame when the rails are on the post will be very near the shape of a boy's hexagonal kite.

Inside erect another set of posts, setting each one opposite the outside ones and about a foot and a half or two feet farther in, or maybe less distance, according to the material one is using.   Next set some posts for the hallway or entrance, which will be the door-jambs, and you are ready to build up the log roof.   Do this by first setting the rail securely on the two side-posts on the right and left of the building; then secure the back plate on the two back posts at the rear of the building, next resting a long log over the side rails at the front of the building.   The door-posts, of course, must be enough taller than the two end posts to allow for the thickness of the log, so that the front log will rest upon their top.   Next put your two corner logs on, and your outside rail is complete.   Build the inside rail in the same manner; then continue to build up with the logs as shown in the diagram until you have a frame like that in Fig. 145.   Fig. 147 shows the inside of the house and the low doorway, and Fig. 148 shows the slanting walls.   This frame is supposed to be covered with splits or shakes (Figs. 147 and 148), but, as in all pioneer structures, if shakes, splits, and clapboards are unobtainable, use the material at hand—birch bark, spruce bark, tar paper, old tin roofing, tent-cloth, or sticks, brush, ferns, weeds, or round sticks, to cover it as you did with the Pawnee hogan (Figs. 42 and 43).   Then cover it with browse, or thatch it with hay or straw and hold the thatch in place with poles or sticks, as shown in Fig. 146.   The barabara may also be covered with earth, sod, or mud.

This sort of a house, if built with planks or boards nailed securely to the rafters and covered with earth and sod, will make a splendid cave house for boys and a playhouse for children on the lawn, and it may be covered with green growing sod so as to have the appearance of an ornamental mound. The instinct of the cave-dweller is deeply implanted in the hearts of boys, and every year we have a list of fatal accidents caused by the little fellows digging caves in sand-banks or banks of gravel which frequently fall in and bury the little troglodytes, but they will be safe in a barabara. The shack is ventilated by a chimney hole in the roof as shown by Fig. 146. This hole should be protected in a playhouse. The framework is a good one to use in all parts of the country for more or less permanent camps, but the long entrance and low doorway are unnecessary except in a cold climate or to add to the mystery of the cave house for children. It is a good form for a dugout for a root house or cyclone cellar.

XXIII

THE NAVAJO HOGAN, HORNADAY DUGOUT, AND SOD HOUSE

I<small>F</small> the reader has ever built little log-cabin traps he knows just how to build a Navajo hogan or at least the particular Navajo hogan shown by Figs. 148 and 150. This one is six-sided and may be improved by notching the logs (Figs. 162, 164, 165) and building them up one on top of the other, dome-shaped, to the required height. After laying some rafters for the roof and leaving a hole for the chimney the frame is complete. In hot countries no chimney hole is left in the roof, because the people there do not build fires inside the house; they go indoors to keep cool and not to get warm; but the Navajo hogan also makes a good cold-country house in places where people really need a fire. Make the doorway by leaving an opening (Fig. 150) and chinking the logs along the opening to hold them in place until the door-jamb is nailed or pegged to them, and then build a shed entranceway (Fig. 153), which is necessary because the slanting sides of the house with an unroofed doorway have no protection against the free entrance of dust and rain or snow, and every section of this country is subject to visits from one of these elements. The house is covered with brush, browse, or sod.

Log Dugout

Fig. 152 shows how to make a log dugout by building the walls of the log cabin in a level place dug for it in the

Forms of dugouts and mound shacks.

bank.   Among the log cabins proper (Figs. 162 and 166) we tell how to notch the logs for this purpose.

Fig. 151 shows one of these log dugouts which I have named the Hornaday from the fact that Doctor William Hornaday happens to be sitting in front of the one represented in the sketch.   Fig. 154 shows a dugout with walls made of sod which is piled up like stones in a stone wall.   The roofs of all these are very flat and made of logs (Figs. 54, 55, and 56), often with a log pegged to the rafters above the eaves to hold the sod.   All such houses are good in dry countries, cold countries, and countries frequented by tornadoes or by winds severe enough to blow down ordinary camps.

The Navajo hogan is an easy sort of a house for boys to build because the lads may use small poles in place of logs with which to build the camp and thus make the labor light enough to suit their undeveloped muscles, but the next illustration shows how to build an American boy's hogan of milled lumber such as one can procure in thickly settled parts of the country.

XXIV

HOW TO BUILD AN AMERICAN BOY'S HOGAN

THE first time any working plans of an underground house for boys were published was when an article by the present writer on the subject appeared in the *Ladies' Home Journal*. Afterward it was published with a lot of similar material in "The Jack of All Trades." Since then other writers have not hesitated to use the author's sketches with very little alteration; imitation is the sincerest compliment, although it is not always fair, but it does, however, show the popularity of the underground-house idea.

The American boy's hogan may be built like the preceding shacks of the material found in the woods or it may be constructed of old boards and waste material to be found in village back yards or on the farm, or, if the boys have the price or if they can interest their fathers or uncles in their scheme, it may be built of milled lumber procured at the lumber-yard.

Frame

Procure some good, sound planks and some pieces of two by four with which to build your frame. The hogan should be large enough to allow room for a table made of a packing-case, some benches, stools, or chairs, and the ceilings should be high enough for the tallest boy to stand erect without bumping his head.

Furniture

One funny thing about this house is that it must be furnished before it is built, because the doorway and passageway will be too small to admit any furniture larger than a stool. Select or make your furniture and have it ready, then decide upon the location of your hogan, which should be, like the Western dugouts, on the edge of some bank (Fig. 158). In this diagram the dotted line shows how the bank originally sloped.

Foundation

The real hard work connected with this is the digging of the foundation; one Y. M. C. A. man started to build one of these hogans, but he "weakened" before he had the foundation dug. He wrote the author a long letter complaining of the hard work; at the same time the author was receiving letters from *boys* telling how much fun they had in building and finishing their underground houses.

Caves

Ever since "Robinson Crusoe" and "Swiss Family Robinson" were written cave houses have been particularly attractive to boys; no doubt they were just as attractive before these books were written, and that may be the reason the books themselves are so popular; at any rate, when the author was a small boy he was always searching for natural caves, or trying to dig them for himself, and so were all of his companions. One of the most charming features of the "Tom Sawyer" and "Huckleberry Finn" stories is that part connected with the cave.

AMERICAN BOYS HOGAN

157

FRONT DOOR WAY

DOOR

157B

157A

157C

156

158

159

NAIL BOARD

160

FRONT VIEW OF ROOF OF HOUSE

155

BANK

EARTH BRUSH

BRUSH

161

VENT

The original American boy's hogan or underground house.

Dangerous Caves

The trouble is that with caves which the boys dig for themselves there is always serious danger of the roof falling in and smothering the young troglodytes, but a properly built underground hogan is perfectly safe from such accidents.

Framing

After you have levelled off the foundation erect the rear posts of two-by-fours *A*, *B* and *C*, *D* (Fig. 156). These posts should be of the same height and tall enough to allow the roof to slant toward the front as in Fig. 155. The front posts *E*, *F* and *G*, *H*, although shorter than the back posts, should be tall enough to allow headroom. One, two, or three more posts may be erected between the post *A*, *B* and the post *C*, *D* if additional strength is required. The same is true of the sides, and in place of having only one post in the middle of each side (*M*, *N* and *O*, *P*, Fig. 156), there may be two or three posts, all according to the size of the house you are building; the main point is to make *a compact and strong box* of your framework so that in the wet weather the banks surrounding it will not be tempted to push in the sides and spoil your house.

Decaying Wood

Locust, chestnut, and cedar will last longer than other varieties of wood when exposed to contact with damp earth, but common wood, which rots easily, may be protected by preservatives, one of which is boiled linseed-oil with pulverized charcoal stirred into it until a black paint is produced. Some people say that a coat of charcoal

paint will preserve even a basswood fence post for a life-
time, and if that is true a hogan protected by a coating
upon the outside of paint made by stirring fine charcoal
into boiled linseed-oil until it is as thick as paint will last
longer than any of my readers will have occasion to use
the hogan for a playhouse. Erect the frame (Fig. 156)
by having some boys hold the uprights in place until they
can be secured with temporary braces like those shown
running diagonally across from *B* to *E* and *A* to *F*. You
may then proceed to board up the sides from the outside
of the frame by slipping the planks between the frame
and the bank and then nailing from the inside wherever
you lack room upon the outside to swing your hammer.
The door-jambs *I*, *J* and *K*, *L* will help support the roof.

The Roof

The roof may be made of lumber, as shown by Fig. 160,
or it may be made of poles like those shown on the Wyoming Olebo (Fig. 236), or it may be made of planks and
covered with tar paper (Figs. 296, 297, 298, and 299), or it
may be shingled, using barrel staves for shingles, or covered with bits of old tin roofing tacked over the planking—or anything, in fact, which will keep out the water.
As for looks, that will not count because the roof is to be
afterward covered with sod.

Cliff-House Roof

If you wish to make the roof as the cliff-dwellers made
theirs, put your biggest logs crosswise from *A*, *M*, *E* to
C, *O*, *G* of your house for rafters, and across the larger
logs lay a lot of small poles as close together as may be,
running from the back to the front of the house. Fill in
the cracks between with moss or calk them with dry

grass; on them place a layer of brush, browse, or small sticks and over this a thick coating of clay, hard-pan, or ordinary mud and pack it down hard by tramping it with your feet until it becomes a smooth and tightly packed crust; over this you can put your sod and weeds to conceal your secret.

Passageway

To make the frame for the underground hall or passageway (Fig. 156), first nail Q, S across the door-jambs to form the top to the doorway, after which put in the supports Q, R and S, T. Next build the frame U, V, X, W and join it to Q, S by the two pieces Q, U and S, V and put in the middle frame support marked $ZZZZ$.

The passageway should be about six feet long and the front doorway (U, V, X, W, Figs. 156 and 157) of sufficient size to enable you to creep through with comfort. The bottom piece W, X can be nailed to a couple of sticks driven in the ground for that purpose. The next thing in order is the floor, and to make this firm you must lay a number of two-by-fours parallel to B, D and F, H and see that they are level. You will need a number of shorter pieces of the same material to run parallel to F, H and W, X for the hall floor, as may be seen in Fig. 157. Across these nail your floor securely as shown in Fig. 155.

There are no windows shown in the diagram, but if the builders wish one it can be placed immediately over the entrance or hallway in the frame marked I, K, Q, S (Fig. 156), in which case the top covering of dirt must be shovelled away from it to admit the light in the same manner that it is in the dugout shown in Fig. 142 and also in the small sketch (Fig. 154). The ventilator shown in Fig. 155 may be replaced, if thought desirable, by a chimney for an open fire. On account of the need of ventilation a stove would not be the proper thing for an underground house, but an open fire would help the ventilation. In the diagram the ventilator is set over a square hole in the roof; it may be made of a barrel or barrels, with the heads knocked out, placed over the hole in the roof, or kegs, according to the size of the roof. When your house is complete fill in the dirt around the edges, pack it down good and hard by the use of a piece of scantling two by four or four by four as a rammer, then cover the roof with small sticks and fine brush and sod it with growing weeds or grass.

The Door

You should have a good, stout front door (Fig. 157) and a padlock with which to secure it from trespassers.

Aures Hinge

A rustic hinge may be made by splitting a forked branch (Fig. 157 C) and using the two pieces nailed to the sides of the door-jambs (Fig. 157 A) to hold the round ends of the rod (Fig. 157 B) run through them. The middle of the B stick is flattened to fit on the surface of the door to which it is nailed. This hinge was invented by Scout Victor Aures of stockade 41144 of Boy Pioneers of America and a description with neat diagrams sent by the inventor to his chief. When all is completed you can conceal the ventilator with dry brush or by planting weeds or shrubs around it, which will not interfere with the ventilation but will conceal the suspicious-looking pipe protruding from the ground. The top of the ventilator should be protected by slats, as in Fig. 161, or by wire netting with about one-quarter-inch mesh in order to keep small animals from jumping or hopping down into your club-house. Of course, a few toads and frogs, field-mice and chipmunks, or even some lizards and harmless snakes would not frighten any real boy, but at the same time they do not want any such creatures living in the same house with them.

Trap-Door

In place of a ventilator or chimney a trap-door may be placed in the roof and used as a secret entrance, access to inside being had by a ladder. A description of an appropriate ladder follows (Figs. 169 and 170).

Fig. 159 shows a rude way to make a chandelier, and as long as your candles burn brightly you may know that the air in your little hogan is pure and fresh. When such a chandelier is used pieces of tin should be nailed above the candles to prevent the heat from burning holes through the roof.

XXV

HOW TO CUT AND NOTCH LOGS

Boys you have now passed through the *grammar school* of shack making, you are older than you were when you began, you have acquired more skill and more muscle, and it is time to begin to handle the woodsman's axe, to handle it skilfully and to use it as a tool with which to fashion anything from a table to a two-story house. None of you is too young to learn to use the axe. General Grant, George Washington, Abraham Lincoln, Billy Sunday—all of them could wield an axe by the time they were eight or nine years old and do it without chopping off their toes or splitting any one else's head open. Remember that every time you hurt yourself with an axe I have a yellow ribbon for you to wear as a "chump mark"; but, joking aside, we must now get down to serious work of preparing the logs in order to build us a little cabin of our own, a log club-house for our gang, or a log camp for our troop of scouts.

Notching Logs

To make the logs hold together at the corners of our cabins it is necessary to lock them in some manner, and the usual way is to notch them. You may cut flat notches like those shown in Fig. 162 and this will hold the logs together, as shown by 162 *E* or you may only flatten the ends, making the General Putnam joint shown in Fig. 163.

This is called after General Putnam because the log cabins at his old camp near my farm at Redding, Conn., are made in this manner. Or you may use the Pike notch which has a wedge-shaped cut on the lower log, as shown by Fig. 164 *J*, made to fit into a triangular notch shown by 164 *H*. When fitted together these logs look like the sketch marked 164 *F* which was drawn from a cabin built in this manner.

But the simplest notch is the rounded one shown by *A*, *B*, and *C* (Fig. 165). When these are locked together they will fit like those shown at Fig. 165 *D*.

Away up North the people dovetail the ends of the logs (Fig. 166) so that their ends fit snugly together and are also securely locked by their dovetail shape. To build a log house, place the two sill logs on the ground or on the foundation made for them, then two other logs across them, as shown in Fig. 168.

Handling the Logs

That the logs may be more easily handled they should be piled up on a skidway which is made by resting the top ends of a number of poles upon a big log or some other sort of elevation and their lower ends upon the ground. With this arrangement the logs may be rolled off without much trouble as they are used.

Chinking

A log cabin built with hardwood logs or with pitch-pine logs can seldom be made as tight as one built with the straight spruce logs of the virgin forests. The latter will lie as close as the ones shown in Fig. 162 *E*, while the former, on account of their unevenness, will have large cracks between them like those shown in Fig. 165 *D*. These cracks may be stopped up by quartering small

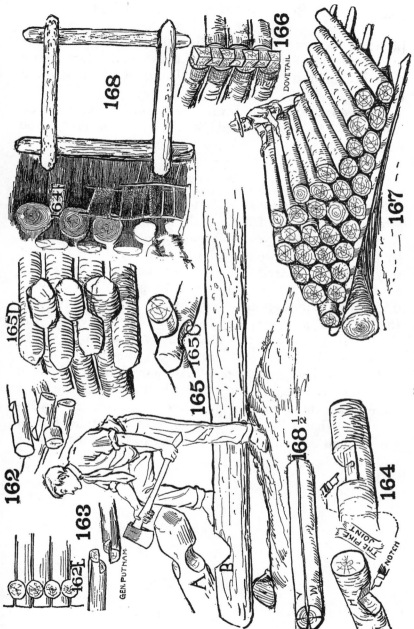

Showing how the logs are notched.

pieces of timber (*Y* and *W*, Fig. 168½) and fitting these quartered pieces into the cracks between the logs where they are held by spikes. This is called "chinking the cabin."

To keep the cold and wind out, the cracks may be "mudded" up on the inside with clay or ordinary lime mortar.

Models

Study these diagrams carefully, then sit down on the ground with a pile of little sticks alongside of you and a sharp jack-knife in your hand and proceed to experiment by building miniature log cabins. Really, this is the best way to plan a large cabin if you intend to erect one. From your model you can see at a glance just how to divide your cabin up into rooms, where you want to place the fireplace, windows, and doors; and I would advise you always to make a small model before building. Make the model about one foot three inches long by ten inches wide, using sticks for logs a little less than one inch in diameter—that is, one inch through or one inch thick. I have taken these dimensions or measurements from a little model that I have before me here in my studio, but, of course, you can vary them according to the plans of your cabin.

XXVI

NOTCHED LOG LADDERS

EVER since man learned to use edged tools he has made ladders or steps, or whatever you may call them, by notching logs (Figs. 169 and 170).

A few years ago I took a splendid trip among the unnamed lakes and in what is known as "the unexplored country"—that is, the unmapped country of northwestern Quebec. We travelled over trails that had not been changed by man since canoes were invented. The forests were untouched by the axe of the white man. There were no roads, no houses, no fences, no people except a few wandering Indians, no cattle except caribou and moose, no dogs except wolves, and we slept at night on beds of balsam and paddled by day through rivers and lakes or carried our luggage and our canoes over the portages from one body of water to another over centuries-old trails. At one place the trail led up the side of a mountain to the beetling face of a cliff—a cliff that we had to climb with all our canoes and luggage, and we climbed it on a couple of notched logs, as shown in Fig. 169. By the way, boys, the Indian with the big load on his back is my old friend Bow-Arrow, formerly chief of the Montainais, and the load on his back was sketched from the real one he carried up that ladder portage. This old man was then sixty years of age. But all this talk is for the purpose of telling you the use of the notched log. Our pioneer ancestors used them to ascend to the loft over

119

170

169

The pioneer log ladder.

their cabins where they slept (Fig. 170). It is also a good ladder to use for tree-houses and a first-rate one for our underground hogans when we have an entrance through the top instead of one at the side shown by Fig. 156. Since you have learned how to use the axe you may make one of these primitive ladders to reach the hay-loft in your barn, if you have a barn. You may make the ladder of one log if you set the pole or log upright and notch it on both sides so that you can clasp it with your hand and, placing one foot on each side of it, climb up in that manner.

XXVII

A POLE HOUSE. HOW TO USE A CROSS-CUT SAW AND A FROE

Pole House

FIG. 171 shows a pole house—that is, a house, the walls of which are made by setting straight poles up on end with sides against each other and nailing a beam across the top (Fig. 172) and toe-nailing them (Fig. 173); that is, driving the nails slantingly down through the poles to the sill beneath. Fig. 172 shows how to nail them to the top beam or side-plate. To build a pole house, erect the four corner-posts and any intermediate posts which may be necessary, nailing the plates on top of the posts to hold the frame together (Fig. 172), afterward fitting the other posts in place, as shown in the sketch.

We have not yet arrived at the part of the book where we can build as extensive houses as the one shown here. The drawing is only inserted at this place because it naturally comes with the use of the cross-cut saw. You can, however, without much trouble, build a small pole house without the veranda, and after you have learned how to build the big log houses you can turn back to this page and try a pole house like Fig. 171.

Sawing on an Angle

Fig. 174 shows how to saw off poles on the bias, as a woman would say, or on an angle, as a man would say.

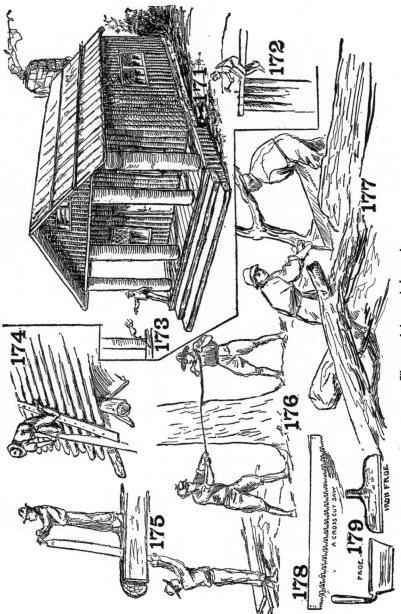

The use of the saw in log work.

Suppose, for instance, you want to cut the poles to fit the dormer over the veranda shown in Fig. 171. Measure off the height of the middle pole, then the distance along the base from the middle pole to the corner at the eaves. Next fit the poles you are going to use closely together to cover that distance; hold them in place by nailing a plank temporarily across the bottom ends; then place another plank at the point marked for the height of the middle pole, run it down to the bottom plank, and nail it temporarily along this line. Now take hold of one end of the saw, as the fellow does in Fig. 174, and let another boy take the other end of the saw; then by working it back and forth along the line you may saw off the protruding ends of the poles. Proceed in the same manner along the base-board. You will then have half the dormer poles all nicely tacked together and cut in the right shape so that they may be evenly fitted in place, and after they are secured there the marking planks may be knocked off. Fig. 175 shows two boys at work "pit-sawing." They are sawing planks from a log, which is rather hard work but not unpleasant. I know, for I have tried it when I was up among the moonshiners in the mountains of Kentucky. Fig. 176 is from a sketch I made up in Michigan, where two men were sawing down a tree as they frequently do nowadays in place of chopping it down with an axe; this tree, however, was first notched with an axe so that it would fall in the right direction. Fig. 178 shows the peculiar teeth of one of these two-handled saws. It is not necessary for you to be expert on the sort of teeth a saw should have; any saw that cuts well for your purpose is the sort of saw you need.

The Froe

Fig. 179 shows two forms of the froe, an implement used for splitting shakes and shingles and clapboards like those on the roof of Fig. 171. The froe is held by the handle with the left hand and hammered on the top with a mallet held in the right hand. Fig. 177 shows two boys sawing a log up into sections, but for our work in cabin building the woodsman's axe is the real tool we need. The saw is all right and may be used if you have it, but it is a little too civilized for real woodcraft work. You cannot throw one of these saws over your shoulder as you would an axe and go marching into the woods with any comfort. The saw is also a more dangerous implement around camp than even a sharp axe.

XXVIII

LOG-ROLLING AND OTHER BUILDING STUNTS

OF course my readers know all about geometry, but if by the rarest of chances one of them should not it will not prevent him from using that science to square the corners of his log cabin. Builders always have a ten-foot measuring rod—that is, a rod or straight stick ten feet long and marked with a line at each foot from end to end. Make your own ten-foot pole of as straight a piece of wood as you can find. With it measure six feet carefully on the log C, G (Fig. 180) and mark the point at O (Fig. 180); measure eight feet on the other log C, A (Fig. 180) and mark the point at N. If these measurements have been carefully made from C to O and from C to N and your corner is "square," then your ten-foot pole will reach between the two points O and N with the tips of the pole exactly touching O and N. If it does not exactly fit between N and O, either the corner is not square or you have not marked off the distances accurately on the logs. Test the measurements and if they are not found true then push your logs one way or the other until it is exactly ten feet from O to N. Then test the corner at H in the same manner.

Log-Rolling

In the olden times log-rolling was always a great frolic and brought the people from far and near to lend a help-

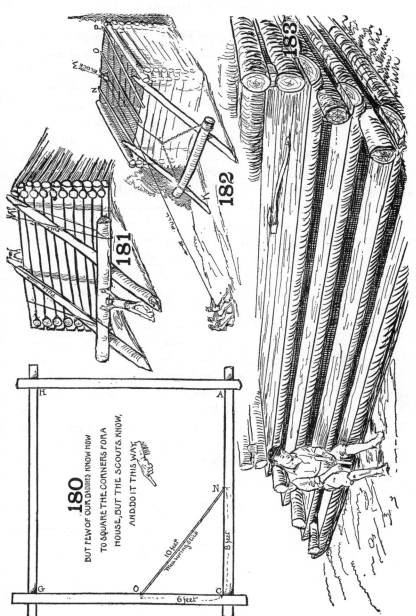

180

BUT FEW OF OUR DADDIES KNOW HOW TO SQUARE THE CORNERS FOR A HOUSE, BUT THE SCOUTS KNOW, AND DO IT THIS WAY

How to square the corners, roll the logs of cabin, and make log steps.

ing hand in building the new house. In handling logs, lumbermen have tools made for that purpose—cant-hooks, peevy irons, lannigans, and numerous other implements with names as peculiar as their looks—but the old backwoodsmen and pioneers who lived in log houses owned no tools but their tomahawks, their axes, and their rifles, and the logs of most of their houses were rolled in place by the men themselves pushing them up the skids laid against the cabin wall for that purpose; later, when the peddlers and traders brought ropes to the settlements, they used these to pull their logs in place. In building my log house in Pennsylvania we used two methods; one was hand power (Fig. 181). Taking two ropes we fastened the ends securely inside the cabin. We then passed the free ends of the ropes around the log, first under it and then over the top of it, then up to a group of men who, by pulling on the free ends, rolled the log (Fig. 181) up to the top of the cabin. But when Lafe Jeems and Nate Tanner and Jimmy Rosencranz were supplied with some oxen they fastened a chain to each end of the log (Fig. 182), then fastened a pulley-block to the other side of the cabin, that is, the side opposite the skids, and ran the line through the pulley-block to the oxen as it is run to the three men in Fig. 182. When the oxen were started the log slid up the skids to the loose rafters *N, O, P* and when once up there it was easily shoved and fitted into place.

Log Steps

Sometimes one wants front steps to one's log house and these may be made of flattened logs or puncheons, as shown by Fig. 183.

XXIX

THE ADIRONDACK OPEN LOG CAMP AND A ONE= ROOM CABIN

Adirondack Log Camp

Not satisfied with the open brush Adirondack camp, the men in those woods often build such camps of logs with a puncheon floor and a roof of real shingles. The sketch (Fig. 184) is made from such a camp. At the rear the logs are notched and placed like those of a log house (Figs. 162, 163, 164, 166), but the front ends of the side logs are toe-nailed (Fig. 173) to the two upright supports. In this particular camp the logs are also flattened on the inside in order to give a smoother finish, as they often are in old Virginia and Kentucky log houses. In Virginia they formerly hewed the logs flat with broad axes after the walls were up, but that required a workman of a different type than the ordinary woodsman. The broadaxe is seldom used now and may be omitted from our kit.

Cabin Plan

A one-room log cabin with double bunks at one end makes a good camp (Fig. 185) with room for two or four sleepers according to the width of the bunk (Fig. 186).

129

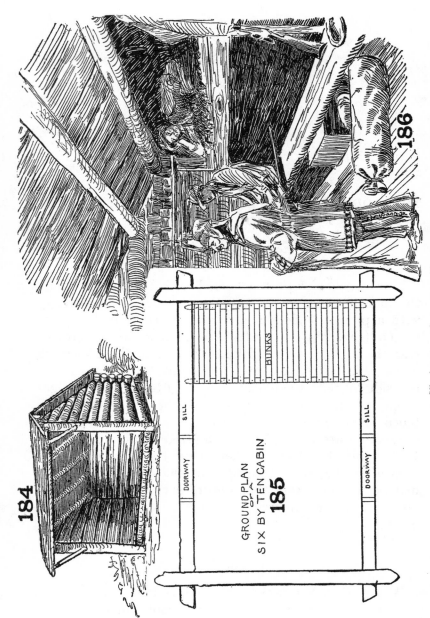

184

GROUND PLAN
OF A
SIX BY TEN CABIN
185

DOORWAY SILL BUNKS SILL DOORWAY

186

The lean-to and one-pen cabin plan.

The Bunks

The bunks are made by setting the ends of two poles into holes in the logs bored for that purpose (Fig. 185) and nailing slats across the poles. Over this a bed of browse is laid and on this blankets are spread and all is then ready for bedtime.

XXX

THE NORTHLAND TILT AND INDIAN LOG TENT

Log Tents

SOME years ago in the north country the Indians built themselves log tents like the one shown in Fig. 187. These were the winter houses in the north country. A ridge-pole was set up on two forked sticks and the logs slanted up against each other and rested upon that pole. Smaller poles were then laid up against this frame, both front and rear, all of which could then be covered with sod or browse and made into a warm winter house. My boy readers may build a similar house by using small poles instead of big logs, or they may make a "northland tilt" (Fig. 189), which is a modification of the Indian's log tent and has two side-plates (Fig. 188) instead of one ridge-pole. The log chimney is also added, and when this is connected with a generous fireplace the fire will brighten and warm the interior of the tilt and make things comfortable. The chimney may be made by first building a fireplace of sod or stone, as shown in Figs. 269 and 270, on top of which a chimney can be erected in the same manner that you build a log house.

The front of the northland tilt is faced in with small logs set on end, as shown in the unfinished one (Fig. 189); this makes a substantial, warm winter camp. If the logs fit close together on the roof they may be calked with moss and dry grass. If the cracks are too wide on ac-

132

A NORTH LAND TILT

188

187

189

INDIAN LOG TENTS
USED FOR WINTER CAMPS
ABOUT, 1820—1850 (IN THE N.WEST)

Log tilts of the North.

count of the unevenness of the log, cover them first with grass, fine brush, or browse and over all place a coating of sod or mud and you will have a house fit for a king to live in.   To tell the truth, it is much too good for a mere king and almost good enough for a real American boy— that is, if anything is good enough for such a lad.

CHAPTER XXXI

HOW TO BUILD THE RED JACKET, THE NEW BRUNS-WICK, AND THE CHRISTOPHER GIST

THE "Red Jacket" is another camp; but this, you see, has straight walls, marking it as *a white man's camp* in form not apparently borrowed from the red men. It is, however, a good, comfortable, rough camp and Figs. 190 and 191 show how it was evolved or grew. To build the Red Jacket one will first have to know how to build the more simple forms which we call the New Brunswick, then the next step will be the Christopher Gist, and last the Red Jacket. We will now begin with the New Brunswick.

The New Brunswick

By referring to Fig. 190 you will see that it is practically a deep, Adirondack, open-face camp with a wind-shield built in front of it. To build this camp, make the plan about six feet by twelve on the ground; of course the back logs must be something over six feet long to allow for six feet in the clear. Notch about four or five back logs with the plain, rounded notch already described and illustrated by Fig. 165. Then lay the side sill logs and erect two upright forked sticks for the front of your cabin to hold the cross stick which supports the roof rafter. Now build up your cabin as you would a log house, notching only the small ends of the side logs and saving the larger ends for the front; between each of these

135

chink with other logs shaped to fit the spaces or with pieces of other logs so as to make the front higher than the rear. When the logs meet the rafter pole all the cracks are chinked up with small pieces of wood and the crevices calked with moss. Then the roof of bark is put on, shingled as described for the Pontiac, and illustrated by Figs. 36 and 190 *A*. The bark is kept in place by laying sticks or poles over it to weight it down, as may be seen by the plan of the roof (Fig. 190 *A*), which is supposed to be the way the unfinished roof would look to you if you were looking down upon it from the branch of a tree or an aeroplane. After you have your open-faced camp finished take some green logs from the fir-trees if they are handy and split them in half by one of the methods shown by Fig. 119. Then leaving enough room for a passage-way, erect your wind-shield of green logs, resting them against a pole laid between two forked sticks. Be sure you have the green, split side of the log facing the camp and the bark side facing outdoors, because the green wood will not burn readily; and as the camp-fire is built close to the wind-shield, if the shield is made of very inflammable material it will soon burn down. Some woods, you know, burn well when green and some woods must be made dry before we can use them for fuel; but the wood we want for the fire-shield is the sort that will not burn readily; the good-burning woods we save to use in our fire.

Christopher Gist

The next camp is the Christopher Gist, named after George Washington's camping friend. This camp, as you may see by Fig. 191, is built like a New Brunswick except that the side sill logs are much longer as is also the log which extends over the doorway. Then, in place of having a wind-shield built by itself, the wind-shield in

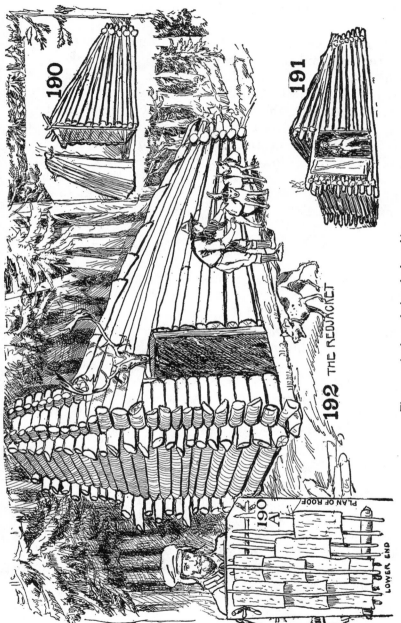

190

191

192 THE REDJACKET

190 A

PLAN OF ROOF

LOWER END

The stages in the evolution of a log cabin.

Fig. 191 is the other end of the cabin built just the same as the rear end, but it should be built of peeled logs as they are less liable to catch afire than the ones with the bark upon them. If you feel real lazy it will only be necessary to peel the bark off from the inside half of the log. Above the door at the end of the roof of the Adirondack camp part of the space is filled by logs running across, with the lower one resting upon the top of the door-jamb; this closes the shed above the wind-shield and leaves a little open yard in front wherein to build your camp-fire.

The Red Jacket

The Red Jacket continues the suggestion offered by the Christopher Gist and extends the side walls all the way across to the wind-shield, and the latter now becomes the true end of the log shack. The side walls and end wall are built up from the top of the shack to form a big, wide log chimney under which the open camp-fire is built on the ground. The Red Jacket is roofed with bark in the same manner as the New Brunswick and Christopher Gist and occupies the important position of the missing link between the true log cabin or log house and the rude log camp of the hunter. If you will look at Fig. 184, the open-faced log camp; then Fig. 190, the camp with the wind-shield in front of it; then Fig. 191 with the wind-shield enclosed but still open at the top; then 192 where the wind-shield has turned into a fireplace with a chimney; then Figs. 271 and 273, showing the ends of the real log cabin, you will have all the steps in the growth or evolution which has produced the American log house.

XXXII

CABIN DOORS AND DOOR-LATCHES, THUMB-LATCHES AND FOOT LATCHES AND HOW TO MAKE THEM

PERHAPS my reader has noticed that, although many of the descriptions of how to build the shacks, shanties, shelters, camps, sheds, tilts, and so forth are given with somewhat minute details, little or nothing has been said regarding the doors and door-latches. Of course we have no doors on the open Adirondack camp, but we have passed the open camps now and are well into cabin work, and all cabins have some sort of a door. All doors have, or should have, some sort of a door-latch, so the doors and door-latches have been saved for this place in the book, where they are sandwiched between the log cabin and the log houses proper, which is probably the best place for them. The "gummers" who collect spruce gum in the north woods and the trappers and all of the hermit class of woodsmen frequently come home to their little shack with their hands full of traps or with game on their shoulders, and consequently they want to have a door which may be opened without the necessity of dropping their load, and so they use a foot latch.

Foot Latch

One of the simplest of the foot latches consists of a piece of wood cut out by the aid of axe and hunting-knife to the form shown by Fig. 199; a hole in the door cut for that purpose admits the flattened and notched end and upon the inside it fits the round log sill. The owner of the shack, when reaching home, steps upon the foot latch (Fig. 199), which lifts up the catch (on the inside) and allows the door to swing open.

Trigger Latch

Fig. 200 shows a more complicated form of latch with a trigger protruding from the lower part of the door, which is hinged to a wooden shaft, and the shaft in turn is connected with the latch. The fastenings of the trigger to the shaft and the shaft to the latch are made with hardwood pegs or wire nails which move freely in their sockets. The latch is the simplest form of a wooden bar fastened at one end with a screw or nail on which it can move up and down freely; the other end is allowed to drop into the catch. The latch itself is similar to the one shown in Figs. 193 and 194. The trigger is also fastened to a block on the outside of the door by a nail or peg upon which it moves freely, so that when the weight of the foot is placed upon the trigger outside the door that end is forced down which pushed the end attached to the shaft up; this pushes the shaft up and the shaft pushes *the latch up;* thus the door is unfastened. The diagram to the left in Fig. 200 shows the edge of the door with the trigger on the outside, the shaft upon the inside. The diagram to the right in Fig. 200 shows the inside of the door, the end of the trigger, the shaft, the latch, and the catch.

The Latch-String

In the preceding locks and fastenings, no matter how generous and hospitable the owner may be, his latch-string

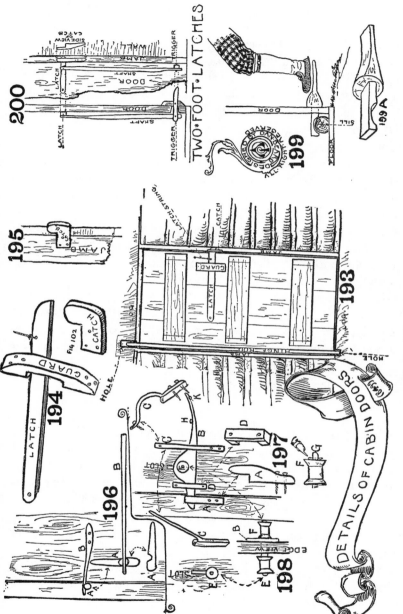

200

SIDE VIEW OF CATCH

JAMB

LATCH

DOOR

TRIGGER

SHAFT

LATCH

DOOR SHAFT

TRIGGER

TWO·FOOT·LATCHES

199

DOOR

FLOOR

SILL

QUALITY RIGHT LADIES DAVE DESERVED

199 A

DOOR

195

JAMB

CATCH

193

LATCH-STRING

JAMB

CATCH

LATCH

GUARD

HINGE ROD

HOLE

194

GUARD

FIG 192

CATCH H

LATCH

HOLE

196

A

B

B

197

K

C

C

H

B

SLOT

D

A

F

G

198

B

F

EDGE VIEW

E

SLOT

DETAILS OF CABIN DOORS

Foot and thumb door-latches.

never "hangs on the outside," but in this one the latch-string literally hangs outside and any one may enter by pulling it (Figs. 193 and 194). But when the owner is in and does not want to be interrupted he pulls the string in, which tells the outsider that he must knock before he can be admitted. This simplest form of latch has been here put upon the simplest form of a door, a door with a wooden hinge made by nailing a round rod to the edge of the door and allowing the ends of the rod to project above and below the door. In the sill log below the door a hole about two inches deep is bored to receive the short end of the hinge rod; above a deeper hole is bored to receive the long end of the hinge rod. To hang the door run the long end up in the top hole far enough to lift the door sufficiently to be able to drop the lower end of the hinge rod in the lower hole. Your door is then hung and may swing back and forth at your pleasure. Notwithstanding the fact that such a door admits plenty of cold air, it is a very popular door for camps and is even used for log houses.

Simple Spring-Latch

A simple form of spring-latch is shown by Fig. 196, as you may see, *A* is a peg driven into the door-jamb. It has a notch in it's outer end so that *B*, a piece of hickory, may be sprung into the notch; *B* is fastened to the door by a couple of screws. By pushing the door the latch will slide out of the rounded notch and the door opens. When you pull the door to close it the end of the spring strikes the rounded end of the *A* peg and, sliding over it, drops naturally into the slot and holds the door closed. This form of latch is also a good one for gates.

Better Spring-Latch

Figs. 197 and 198 show more complicated spring-latches but this latch is not so difficult to make as it may appear in the diagram. *A* and *D* (197) show, respectively, the wooden catch and the guard confining the latch. *C* is another guard made, as you may observe, from a twig with a branch upon it; the twig is split in half and fastened at the base with two screws, and at the upper end, where the branch is bent down, is fastened with one screw. A guard like the one shown by *D* (Fig. 197) would answer the purpose, but I am taking the latch as it was made. The lower diagram (Fig. 198) shows a side view of the edge of the door with two cotton spools fastened at each end of the stick which runs through a slot in the door. *E* is the cotton spool on the outside of the door and *F* the cotton spool on the inside of the door. The upper left-hand diagram (Fig. 198) shows the slot in the door and the spool as it appears from the outside. *B* (Fig. 197) is the spring-latch which is held in place by the spool *F*. The stick or peg which runs through the spools and the slot also runs through a hole made for that purpose in the spring-latch, as shown at *F* (Fig. 197). After the stick with the *E* spool on it has been run through the slot from the outside of the door, thence through the spring-latch *B* and into the spool *F*, it is fastened there by driving around its end some thin wedges of wood or by allowing it to protrude and running a small peg through the protruding end, as shown by *F*, *G* (Fig. 197, lower diagram). The thin, springy end of your latch is now forced down by a peg or nail in the door at *H* (Fig. 197) and the tail end of it forced up by a peg or nail at *K*. When this is done properly it will give considerable spring to the latch and impart a decided tendency to force the latch into the wooden catch, a tendency which can only be overcome by lifting the spool up in the slot and thus lifting the latch and allowing the door to open.   Fig. 197 shows the inside of the door with the spring-latch, catches and all complete; it also gives details of the wooden catch *A* with guards *D* and *C* and the fastening of the stick in the spool by a peg driven through the end of the stick at *F*, *G*.   This last one is a good jack-knife latch to make for your camp or cabin.

XXXIII

SECRET LOCKS

SECRET locks are more useful than strong ones for a country house which is left alone during the winter months, for it is not so much cupidity which causes such houses to be broken into as it is the curiosity of the native boys. But while these lads often do not hesitate to force or pick a lock they will seldom go as far as to smash a door to effect an entrance; hence, if your lock is concealed your house is safe from all but professional thieves, and such gentry seldom waste their time to break open a shack which contains nothing of value to them. The latches shown by Figs. 193, 200, and 201 may be made very heavy and strong, and if the trigger in Fig. 200, the latch-string hole in Fig. 193, and the peg hole in Fig. 201 are adroitly concealed they make the safest and most secure locks for summer camps, shacks, and houses.

If a large bar (Fig. 201½ B) be made of one-by-four-inch plank, bolted in the middle of the plank with an iron bolt through the centre of the door and fastened on the inside by a nut screwed on to the bolt it will allow the bar to revolve freely on the inside of the door and bar the door when resting in the A and C catches. But if a string is attached to one end it may be unfastened by pulling the string up through the gimlet hole in the door.

To conceal this lock, draw the string through the gimlet hole and fasten a nail on the string. When it is un-

145

drawn the door bar is horizontal and the door consequently barred. Then push the nail in the gimlet hole so that only the head appears on the outside and no one not in the secret will ever suppose that the innocent-appearing nail is the key to unfasten the door. When you wish to open the door from the outside, pluck out the nail, pull the string, and walk in.

There are a thousand other simple contrivances which will suggest themselves to the camper, and he can find entertainment for rainy days in planning and enlarging on the ideas here given. In the real wilderness, however, every camp is open to all comers—that is, the latch-string hangs outside the door, but the real woodsmen respect the hospitality of the absent owner and replace whatever food they may use with fresh material from their own packs, wash all dishes they may use, and sweep up and leave the shack in "apple-pie" order after their uninvited visit, for this is the law of the wilderness which even horse thieves and bandits respect.

The Tippecanoe

The Tippecanoe latch is worked with a wooden spring and when properly made, of well-seasoned wood, will probably outlast a metal one, for wood will not rust and cannot rot unless subjected to moisture.

The position of the spring in Fig. 201 shows the latch with the bolt sprung back. The fact that the bolt-hole in the catch is empty also tells the same story. The drawing of the outside of the door (Fig. 203) shows by the position of the peg that the door is fastened. To open the door, push back the bolt by sliding the peg to the opposite end of the slot. From a view of the edge of the door (Fig. 202) one may see how the peg protrudes on the outside of the door.

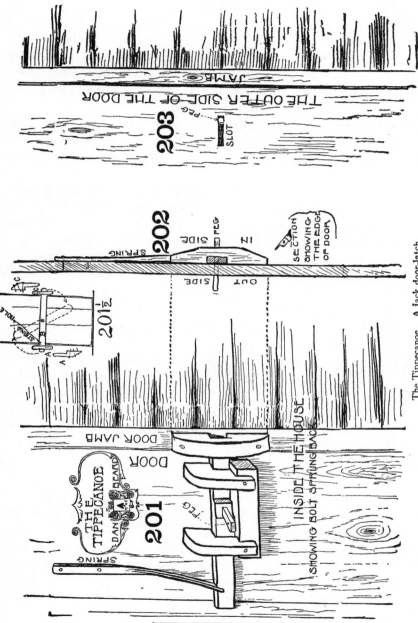

The Tippecanoe. A jack door-latch.

Although the Tippecanoe latch is made of quite a number of parts, it is really a very simple device, but in order to display the simplicity of its construction to the ambitious jack-knife latch maker I have drawn all the parts but the spring stick natural size (Figs. 204 to 207), but since the original diagram is drawn too large for this page and was reduced by the engraver there is a scale of inches at the bottom to give the reader the proportions.

There are no fixed dimensions for this or any other lock, latch, or catch, but the proportions here given are probably the ones that will fit your door. The foundation block is shown by Fig. 204. Upon this the latch rests and is securely nailed or screwed to the door. Figs. 205 and 206 are two wooden clamps which are fastened to the door and also to the foundation block (Fig. 204). These clamps must be notched as in the diagrams to allow for the movement of the bolt, but since the bolt (Fig. 207) is larger and thicker at the butt the notch in Fig. 205 is made just a trifle larger than the butt end of the bolt and in Fig. 206 the notch is made a trifle smaller than the opposite end of the bolt. The object of the offset on the bolt (Fig. 207) forward of the peg is to make a shoulder to stop it from shooting too far when the spring is loosened.

The Catch

Figs. 201 and 204½ show the catch which is to be securely fastened to the door-jamb. The spring, of course, must be made of well-seasoned, elastic wood. Hickory is the best. This stick may be quite long, say half again as long in proportion as the one shown in Fig. 201. It must be flattened at the upper end and secured by two nails and it must be flattened at right angles to the upper part and

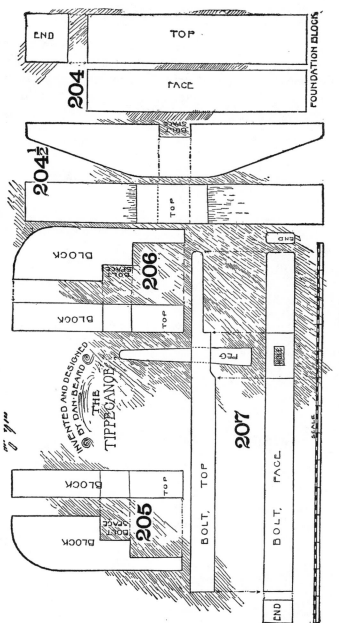

Detail parts of Tippecanoe door-latch.

somewhat pointed at the lower end so as to fit in a notch in the bolt (Fig. 201). A well-made lock of this sort is a source of constant joy and pride to the maker and he will never tire of springing it back and forth and extolling its virtues to his guests.

XXXIV

HOW TO MAKE THE BOW-ARROW CABIN DOOR AND LATCH AND THE DEMING TWIN BOLTS, HALL, AND BILLY

FIG. 209 shows the inside of the door with the wooden latch in place. You may use planks from the sawmill for the door in place of splitting them from spruce logs, as the ones here are supposed to be.

The battens (A, B, C) are made of birch, but you may use any material at hand for them. The hinges (Figs. E, 211 D, 210) are made of birch sticks whittled off at the top so as to leave a peg (Fig. E, 211) to work in a hole in the flattened end of the horizontal battens (A and C, Fig. 209).

The batten B is in two pieces. The top piece serves as a brace for the spring (Fig. G, 209) and the bottom piece as a support for the bolt (Fig. H, 209 and 212). The battens may be made of a piece of board. The bolt (Fig. H, 212) works free upon a nail in the left-hand end and rests in the catch (Fig. K, 215) on the door-jamb.

The guard (Fig. J, 216) fits over the bolt and keeps it in place. The notch in the guard must be long enough to give the bolt free play up and down.

The spring (Fig. G, 209) is fastened with a nail to the door in such a manner that its thin end rests upon the top of the bolt with sufficient force to bend the spring and hold the bolt down in the catch (Fig. K, 215).

The thumb-latch (Fig. *L*, 213) is whittled out in the form shown, and fastened in a slot cut in the door by a nail driven through the edge of the door (Fig. *M*, 213) and through a hole in the thumb-latch (Fig. *L*, 213). On this nail the latch works up and down.

Fig. 217 shows the outside of the door and you can see that by pressing down the thumb-latch on the outside it will lift it up on the inside, and with it the bolt lifts up the free end of the latch and thus unfastens the door.

The handle (Figs. 217 and 214 *N*) is used in place of a door-knob. It is made of yellow birch bent in hot water.

The Deming Twin Lock

E. W. Deming, the painter of Indian pictures, the mighty hunter, and fellow member of the Camp-Fire Club of America, is a great woodsman. Not only is he a great woodsman but he is the father of *twins*, and so we have thought that he possesses all the characteristics necessary to entitle him to a place in this book, and after him and his twins we have named the twin bolts shown by Fig. 208.

The lower or Hall bolt is shot into a hole in the door-sill, and the upper or Billy bolt is shot into a hole in the door-jamb above the door. The holes should be protected upon the surface of the wood by pieces of tin or sheet iron with holes cut in them to admit the bolt. The tins may be tacked over the bolt-hole in the sill for the Hall bolt and on the bolt-hole overhead for the Billy bolt, and it will prevent the splitting away of the wood around the holes.

Guards

Two guards, *A* and *B* (Fig. 208), made as in Fig. 216, protect the bolts and act as guides to keep them from

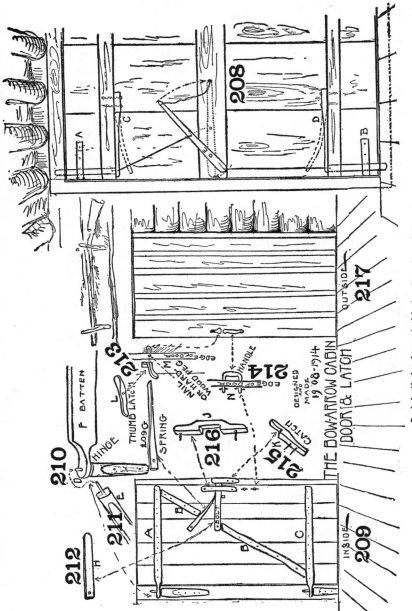

Jack-knife latches suitable for Canada and America.

swinging out of position; two springs *C* and *D* (Fig. 208), made of well-seasoned hickory and attached to the battens on the door by nails or screws, force the bolts down and up into the bolt-holes (Fig. 208). To release the bolts, the spring must be drawn back as shown by the dotted lines in Fig. 208. This may be done by means of a string or picture wire, which is fastened in the ends of the bolts and runs through a hole in the ends of the spring and is attached to the lever *E* (Fig. 208). When the end of this lever is pushed down into the position shown by the dotted line and arrow-point, it lifts up the Hall bolt at the bottom of the door and pulls down the Billy bolt overhead, thus unfastening the door.

But, of course, if one is outside the door one cannot reach the lever *E;* so, to overcome this difficulty, a hole is bored through the central batten of the door and the latch-string is tied to the top end of the lever and the other end is run through the hole bored in the door (Fig. 208).

The end outside of the door is then tied to a nail; by pulling the nail you pull down the lever *E*, which undoes the bolts and opens the door.

When it is desired to leave the door locked, after it is closed, push the nail into the latch-string hole so that only the head will be visible from the outside. When the nail and string are arranged in this manner, a stranger will see no means of opening the door, and, as there are many nail-heads in all rough doors, the one to which the latch-string is attached will not attract the attention of any one who is unacquainted with the Deming twin bolt.

XXXV

THE AURES LOCK LATCH

THE Aures lock differs from the preceding ones in the use of metal springs, but wooden ones may be substituted; for instance, a wooden spring like the one in Fig. 209 may be put under the bolt or latch shown in Fig. 219, which is practically the same latch; that is, if you turn the latch in Fig. 209 upside down it will make the latch shown in Fig. 219; also, if you take the bolt or lock *B* in Fig. 219 and make it of one piece of wood with a spring to it, like the one shown in Fig. 208 or Fig. 209, or make it exactly like the one shown in Fig. 201, the Aures lock can be made altogether of wood. But with this lock, as described below, metal springs were used (Figs. 219, 220, and 221).

The Door

The door shows the two strings *H* and *K* coming through gimlet holes near the top. Fig. 218 represents the outside of the door. The strings may be concealed by covering their ends with a board as shown in this diagram, but even if they are not concealed, one unacquainted with the lock will not know how to work them in order to open the door.

A in Figs. 219, 220, and 221 is the latch which is made of a piece of wood about eight or nine inches long by about one and one half inches wide by an inch or three quarters of an inch thick. A hole is drilled near the centre

155

of the latch and a screw placed through which is screwed into the door so that the latch will extend about two or three inches beyond the end of the door.

D (Figs. 219, 220, and 221) is a catch or stop which is fastened to the door-jamb and keeps the end of the latch from flying too far up to lock the door.

B (Fig. 219) is the key which is made of the same sort of wood as the latch; a hole is drilled in this also but it is here placed about one inch from the top. A screw is run through this, as in the hole in the latch, and screwed into the door (Fig. 219).

Fig. *C*, 219 is a small block of wood on which a steel-band spring has been screwed to keep the key in its proper place. The block is screwed to the door a short distance above the top of the key.

Fig. *J*, 219 is a nail or peg placed in the door close beside the key when the key is vertical; this is intended to prevent the key from being shoved over too far by the force of the band spring *F*.

Fig. 219 *L* is a steel wire spring (a window-shade spring will answer the purpose), fastened to the door at one end and to the latch at the other end, and serves to keep the latch down and in place when locked.

Fig. 219 *K* is the latch-string, one end of which is fastened to one end of the latch and the other end run through a hole near the top of the door and extending outside the same as the latch-string (Fig. 218).

Fig. 219 shows the positions of the latch and key when the latch is locked; to open the lock from the outside it is necessary to pull the key string first (*H*, Fig. 220), which releases the key; then pull the latch-string, thus lifting the latch while still holding the key string. The key string is now let go; the spring forcing the key into the position shown in Fig. 221 will keep the door unlocked.

When leaving the room, all that is necessary is to pull

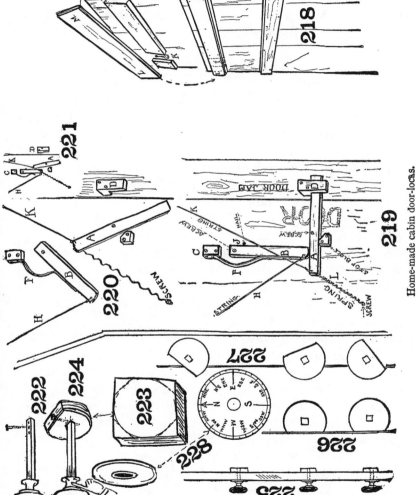

Home-made cabin door-locks.

the key string which lifts the key, then let go the latch-string, and the latch will spring back to its locked position and the key will also fly back into its position as in Fig. 219. Any one not knowing the combination will be unable to open the door.

The Compass Lock

This lock is made on the same principle as the combination safe lock, but it is a lock any bright boy can make for himself. In the first place, instead of numbers, use compass divisions; that is, use a disk with the points of the compass scratched on it and an ordinary door-knob with an index mark filed on its base, as shown by Fig. 224 where the finger is pointing.

Hunt up three old door-knobs like those shown in Figs. 222, 224, and 225. When you take one of the door-knobs off one end of the shaft you will find several small screw holes in the steel shaft (Fig. 222). Over this end you set a block of hardwood which you fashion out of a square block (Fig. 223) by first cutting off the corners as shown by the dotted lines, then whittling the angles off until it becomes rounded like a compass face; after which saw off an arc, that is, part of a circle, as shown in Figs. 224, 226, and 227. Next make a square hole through the centre of the circle to fit the square end of the steel shaft of the door-knob. The square hole is not the centre of the block as it is now cut, but it is the centre of the block as it was when it was round; that is, the centre of the circle. Insert the square end of the steel shaft into the square hole in the block, and, through a hole carefully drilled for the purpose, put a screw down through the hole in the end of the steel shaft (Fig. 224); this will firmly fix the block on the end of the knob. Of course, the knob must be inserted through the door before the block is permanently fastened upon the end of the shaft. Fig. 225 shows the edge of the door with the three knobs in place. If these knobs are so turned (Fig. 226) that their flat edges are parallel with the crack of the door, there is nothing to prevent you from opening the door; but if the knobs are so turned (Fig. 227) that the blocks overlap the crack of the door, the door cannot be opened without breaking the lock.

It is evident that we must have some sort of a mark to tell us how to make the proper combination so that the door may be opened. To do this, take the metal washer of the door-knob (the upper figure in Fig. 228) or a circular piece or disk of tin and divide it up like a compass (Fig. 228). Fasten these disks securely on to the door with nails or screws; place all of the disks with the north point pointing to the top of the door and in line with each other. File in the circular base of each door-knob (Fig. 224) a little notch at the black mark where the finger is pointing, then put the door-knobs in place and fasten them there (Fig. 225) by screwing the block on their ends (Fig. 224) and securing the screws in the blocks by running them through the shaft. Carefully turn the knobs so that the block on the inside fits like those shown in Fig. 226. Jot down in your notebook the position of the index on each knob (finger point, 224); one may read northeast, another may read southwest, and another may read south. When one wants to open the door one must turn the knobs so that they will read according to the notes and the door may be opened; but unless the indexes read as noted some of them will be turned as in Fig. 227, locking the door, and it may not be opened.

When the door is closed, twist the knobs around and it will lock them so that no one else can open the door unless they know the combination. The fact that there *is* a combination will not be suggested to a stranger by the compasses, although it might be suggested if there were figures in place of compass points. But even supposing they did suspect a combination it would take a long time for them to work it out, and no one would do it but a thief. A burglar, however, would not take the time; he would pry open the door with his "jimmy" and, as I have said before, these locks are for the purpose of keeping out tramps, vagrants, and inquisitive boys.

We have no locks yet invented which will keep out a real, professional burglar if he has reason to suppose there are valuables inside.

The safety of your log cabin depends principally upon the fact that valuables are not kept in such shacks, and real burglars know it.

XXXVI

THE AMERICAN LOG CABIN

Now that we know how to make doors and door-latches, locks, bolts, and bars, we may busy ourselves with building an American log cabin. It is all well enough to build our shacks and shanties and camps of logs with the bark on them, but, when one wishes to build a log cabin, one wants a house that will last. Abraham Lincoln's log cabin is still in existence, but it was built of logs with no bark on them. There is a two-story log house still standing in Dayton, O.; it is said to have been built before the town was there; but there is no bark on the logs. Bark holds moisture and moisture creates decay by inviting fibrous and threadlike cousins of the toadstool to grow on the damp wood and work their way into its substance. The bark also shelters all sorts of boring insects and the boring insects make holes through the logs which admit the rain and in the end cause decay, so that the first thing to remember is to peel the logs of which you propose to build the cabin. There is now, or was lately, a log cabin on Hempstead Plains, L. I., near the road leading from Mineola to Manhassett; it is supposed to have been built when the first white settlers began to arrive on Long Island, but this was what was known as a "blockhouse," a small fort. In 1906 Mr. I. P. Sapington said: "I think that I am the only man now living who helped build General Grant's log cabin." Grant's house was what is popularly known in the South as a "saddle-bag" log house, or, as the old Southwestern settlers called it, a "two-pen," the pens being two enclosures with a wide passageway or gallery between them, one roof extending over both pens and the gallery.

General Grant was not afraid of work, and, like a good scout, was always willing to help a neighbor. He had a team of big horses, a gray and a bay, and the loads of cord-wood he hauled to St. Louis were so big that they are still talked of by the old settlers. In the summer of 1854 Grant started his log cabin, and all his neighbors turned in to help him build his house.

American Log House

The American log house differs from the Canadian log house principally in the shape of the roof. Our old settlers made steep gambrel roofs to shed the rain.

"Gambrel! Gambrel? Let me beg
You'll look at a horse's hinder leg;
First great angle above the hoof,
That's the gambrel, hence the gambrel roof."

The Canadians put very flat roofs on their log cabins, usually composed of logs laid over the rafters, making them strong enough to support the heavy weight of snow. The American log cabins, as a rule, are built in a milder climate, and the flat sod roof is peculiar to our Northern boundary and the hot, arid parts of our country. We build the chimneys outside of our log cabins because, as the old settlers would say, "thar's more room out thar" (see Figs. 271, 273).

One-Pen Cabin

Fig. 229 is a one-pen cabin. To build it we first snake our logs to a skid near the site of our proposed cabin

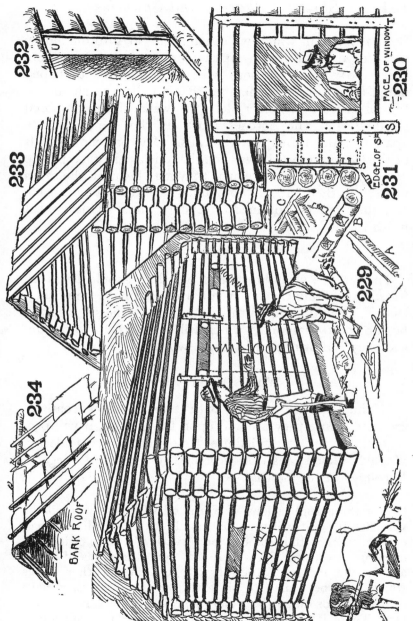

Hints and suggestions in cabin construction.

(Fig. 167), from which we can roll our logs to our house as we need them. Lay out the corners and square them (Fig. 180); notch the logs with a rounded or U-shaped notch (Fig. 165). Remember that all the logs should be two or three feet longer than the walls of the proposed building, but the notches must be the same distance apart in order to make even walls. The protruding ends of the logs may be allowed to stick out as they happen to come, no matter how irregular they may be, until the cabin is erected; then with a two-handed saw and a boy at each end they can be trimmed off evenly, thus giving a neat finish to the house.

Sills

The largest, straightest, and best logs should be saved for sills or foundations. If you are building a "mudsill," that is, a building upon the ground itself, the sill logs will be subject to dampness which will cause them to rot unless they are protected by some wood preservative.

Wood Preservative

If the logs are painted with two or three coats of creosote before they are laid upon the ground, it will protect them for an indefinite time and prevent decay. Hugh P. Baker, dean of the New York State College of Forestry, writes me that—

two or three applications of warm oil with a brush will be very helpful and will probably be all that the ordinary man can do. Creosote is the best preservative because of its penetrating power and the way it acts upon the fibres of wood, and in the end is cheaper than a good many other things which have been used to preserve timber. In fact, various forms of creosote are best-known preservers of organic matter. There is no advantage in using charcoal at all and I presume suggestions have been made for using it because we know that charred wood is more durable. Linseed-oil is good; ordinary white-lead paint will be better, but neither of them is as effective as creosote, and both are more expensive. You will find that carbolineum and other patent preparations are recommended very highly; they are good but expensive and the difference in price between these patent preparations and ordinary creosote is much larger than is justified by their increased value. Creosote can be procured in large or small quantities from a number of concerns. I think we have been getting it for about ten dollars per barrel of fifty or fifty-three gallons.

Creosote

may be purchased in large or small quantities from various manufacturing companies, such as the Barret Manufacturing Company, 17 Battery Place, New York City, and the Chattfield Manufacturing Company, Carthage, O., handle it in large quantities.

Openings

Build the pen as if it were to have no openings, either doors, windows, or fireplaces. When you reach the point where the top of the door, window, or fireplace is to be (Fig. 229) saw out a section of the log to mark the place and admit a saw when it is desired to finish the opening as shown in the diagram and continue building until you have enough logs in place to tack on cleats like those shown in Figs. 229, 230, and 231, after which the openings may be sawed out. The cleats will hold the ends of the logs in place until the boards U (Fig. 232) for the door-jambs, window-frames, or the framework over the fireplace can be nailed to the ends of the logs and thus hold them permanently in place. If your house is a "mudsill," wet the floor until it becomes spongy, then

with the butt end of a log ram the dirt down hard until
you have an even, hard floor—such a floor as some of the
greatest men of this nation first crept over when they were
babies. But if you want a board floor, you must necessarily have floor-joists; these are easily made of milled lumber or you may use the rustic material of which your house
is built and select some straight logs for your joists. Of
course, these joists must have an even top surface, which
may be made by flattening the logs by scoring and hewing
them as illustrated by Figs. 123, 124, and 125 and previously described. It will then be necessary to cut the
ends of the joist square and smaller than the rest of the log
(Fig. *A*, 229); the square ends must be made to fit easily
into the notches made in the sill logs (*B*, Fig. 229) so
that they will all be even and ready for the flooring
(*C*, Fig. 229). For a house ten feet wide the joists should
be half a foot in diameter, that is, half a foot through
from one side to the other; for larger spans use larger
logs for the joists.

Foundation

If your house is not a "mudsill" you may rest your
sill logs upon posts or stone piles; in either case, in the
Northern States, they should extend three feet below
the ground, so as to be below frost-line and prevent the
upheaval of the spring thaw from throwing your house
"out of plumb."

Roofing

All the old-time log cabins were roofed with shakes,
splits, clapboards, or hand-rived shingles as already described and illustrated by Figs. 126, 128, 129, and 130;
but to-day they are usually shingled with the machine-
sawed shingle of commerce. You may, however, cover
the roof with planks as shown by Fig. 233 or with bark

weighted down with poles as shown by Fig. 234. In covering it with board or plank nail the latter on as you would on a floor, then lay another course of boards over the cracks which show between the boards on the first course.

Gables

The gable ends of the cabin should be built up of logs with the rafters of the roof running between the logs as they are in Figs. 229 and 233, but the roof may be built, as it frequently is nowadays, of mill lumber, in which case it may be framed as shown by Figs. 49, 51, and the gable end above the logs filled in with upright poles as shown in Figs. 173 and 247, or planked up as shown in the Southern saddle-bag (Fig. 241), or the ends may be boarded up and covered with tar paper as shown in Fig. 248, or the gable end may be shingled with ordinary shingles (Fig. 79).

Steep Roof

Remember that the steeper the roof is the longer the shingles will last, because the water will run off readily and quickly on a steep surface and the shingles have an opportunity to dry quickly; besides which the snow slides off a steep roof and the driving rains do not beat under the shingles. If you are using milled lumber for the roof, erect the rafters at the gable end first, with the ridge board as shown in Fig. 263 and in greater detail in Fig. 49. Put the other rafters two or three feet apart.

Let your roof overhang the walls by at least seven or eight inches so as to keep the drip from the rain free of the wall. It is much easier for the architect to draw a log house than it is for a builder to erect one, for the simple reason that the draughtsman can make his logs as straight as he chooses, also that he can put the uneven places where they fit best; but except in well-forested countries the tree trunks do not grow as straight as the logs in my pictures and you must pick out the logs which will fit together. Run them alternately butt and head; that is, if you put the thick end of the log at the right-hand end of your house, with the small end at the left, put the next log with the small end at the right and thick end at the left; otherwise, if all the thick ends are put at one side and the small ends at the other, your house will be taller at one end than at the other as is the case with some of our previous shacks and camps (Figs. 190, 191, and 192) which are purposely built that way.

If it is planned to have glass window lights, make your window openings of the proper size to fit the window-frames which come with the sashes from the factory. In any case, if the cabin is to be left unoccupied you should have heavy shutters to fit in the window opening so as to keep out trespassers.

Chinking

If your logs are uneven and leave large spaces between them, they may be chinked up by filling the spaces with mud plaster or cement, and then forcing in quartered pieces of small logs and nailing them or spiking them in position. If your logs are straight spruce logs and fit snugly, the cracks may be calked up with swamp moss (Sphagnum), or like a boat, with oakum, or the larger spaces may be filled with flat stones and covered with mud. This mud will last from one to seven or eight years; I have some on my own log cabin that has been there even a longer time.

XXXVII

A HUNTER'S OR FISHERMAN'S CABIN

In all the hilly and mountainous States there are tracts of forest lands and waste lands of no use to the farmer and of no use to settlers, but such places offer ideal spots for summer camps for boys and naturalists, for fishermen and sportsmen, and here they may erect their cabins (*see Frontispiece*) and enjoy themselves in a healthy, natural manner. These cabins will vary according to the wants of the owners, according to the material at hand and the land upon which they are built. By extending the rafters of the roof, the latter may be extended (*see Frontispiece*) to protect the front and make a sort of piazza which may be floored with puncheons.

The logs forming the sides of the house may be allowed to extend so as to make a wall or fence, as they do on the right-hand side of the Frontispiece, thus preventing the danger of falling over the cliff upon which this cabin is perched and receiving injury or an unlooked-for ducking in the lake. They may also be extended as they are on the left, to make a shield behind which a wood-yard is concealed, or to protect an enclosure for the storage of the larger camp utensils.

In fact, this drawing is made as a suggestion and not to be copied exactly, because every spot differs from every other spot, and one wants to make one's house conform to the requirements of its location; for instance, the logs upon the right-hand side might be allowed to extend all the way up to the roof, as they do at the bottom, and thus make a cosey corner protected from the wind and storm.

The windows in such a cabin may be made very small, for all work is supposed to be done outdoors, and when more light is needed on the inside the door may be left open. In a black-fly country or a mosquito country, however, when you are out of reach of screen doors, mosquito-netting may be tacked over the windows and a portière of mosquito-netting over the doorway.

XXXVIII

HOW TO MAKE A WYOMING OLEBO, A HOKO RIVER OLEBO, A SHAKE CABIN, A CANADIAN MOSSBACK, AND A TWO-PEN OR SOUTHERN SADDLE-BAG HOUSE

ONE of the charms of a log-cabin building is the many possibilities of novelties suggested by the logs themselves. In the hunter's cabin (*see Frontispiece*) we have seen how the ends of the logs were allowed to stick out in front and form a rail for the front stoop; the builders of the olebos have followed this idea still further.

The Wyoming Olebo

In Fig. 236 we see that the side walls of the pen are allowed to extend on each side so as to enclose a roofed-over open-air room, or, if you choose to so call it, a front porch, veranda, stoop, piazza, or gallery, according to the section of the country in which you live.

So as to better understand this cabin the plan is drawn in perspective, with the cabin above and made to appear as if some one had lifted the cabin to show the ground-floor plan underneath. The olebo roof is built upon the same plan as the Kanuck (Fig. 244), with this exception, that in Fig. 244 the rooftree or ridge-log is supported by cross logs which are a continuation of the side of the house (*A, A,* Figs. 242, 244, and 245), but in the olebo the ridge

pole or log is supported by uprights (Figs. 236 and 237).
To build the olebo lay the two side sill logs first (*A, B,*
and *C, D,* Fig. 236), then the two end logs *E, F,* and *D, B*
and proceed to build the cabin as already described, allowing the irregular ends of the logs to extend beyond the
cabin until the pen is completed and all is ready for the
roof, after which the protruding ends of the logs *excepting
the two top ones* may be sawed off to suit the taste and
convenience of the builder. The olebo may be made of
any size that the logs will permit and one's taste dictate.
After the walls are built, erect the log columns at *A* and *C*
(Fig. 236), cut their tops wedge shape to fit in notches in
the ends of the projecting side-plates (Fig. 144, *A* and *B*);
next lay the end plate (*G,* Fig. 236) over the two top logs
on the sides of your house which correspond to the side-
plates of an ordinary house. The end plate *G* is notched
to fit on top of the side-plates, and the tops of the side-
plates have been scored and hewn and flattened, thus
making a General Putnam joint like the one shown above
(*G,* Fig. 236); but when the ends of the side logs of the
cabin were trimmed off the side-plates or top side logs were
allowed to protrude a foot or more beyond the others; this
was to give room for the supporting upright log columns
at *A* and *C* (see view of cabin, Fig. 236 and the front
view, Fig. 237). *H* and *J* (Fig. 237) are two more upright
columns supporting the end plate which, in turn, supports
the short uprights upon which the two purlins *L* and *M*
rest; the other purlins *K* and *N* rest directly upon the
end plate (Fig. 237). The rear end of the cabin can have
the gable logged up as the front of the house is in Fig.
240, or filled in with uprights as in Fig. 247. The roof of
the olebo is composed of logs, but if one is building an
olebo where it will not be subjected during the winter to
a great weight of snow, one may make the roof of any
material handy.

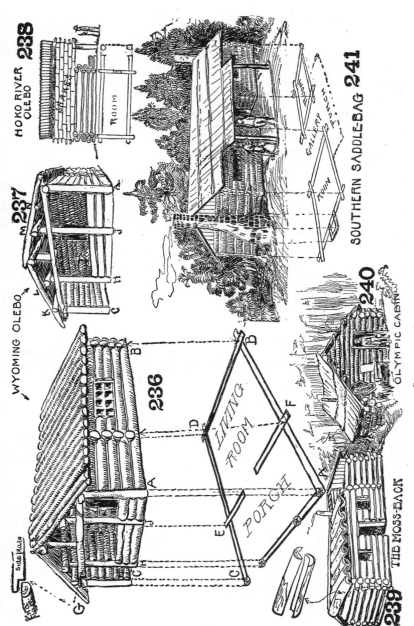

237 WYOMING OLEBO

238 HOKO RIVER OLEBO

SHAKE

ROOM

236

LIVING ROOM

PORCH

239 THE MOSS-BACK

240 OLYMPIC CABIN

241 SOUTHERN SADDLE-BAG

GALLERY PORCH

ROOM

Side plate

Some native American log houses,

Hoko River Olebo

The Hoko River olebo has logs only up to the ceiling
of the first story (Fig. 238), or the half story as the case
may be; this part, as you see, is covered with shakes previously illustrated and described (Figs. 127, 128, 129, and
130). The logs supporting the front of the second story
serve their purpose as pillars or supports only during the
winter-time, when the heavy load of snow might break off
the unsupported front of the olebo. In the summer-time
they are taken away and set to one side, leaving the
overhang unsupported in front. The shakes on the side
are put on the same as shingles, overlapping each other
and breaking joints as shown in the illustration. They
are nailed to the side poles, the ends of which you may
see protruding in the sketch (Fig. 238).

The Mossback Cabin

In the north country, where the lumbermen are at
work, the farmers or settlers are looked down upon by
the lumberjacks much in the same manner as the civilians in a military government are looked down upon by
the soldiers, and hence the lumberjacks have, in derision,
dubbed the settlers mossbacks.

Mossback

Fig. 239 shows a mossback's house or cabin in the
lake lands of Canada. The same type of house I have
seen in northern Michigan. This one is a two-pen house,
but the second pen is made like the front to the olebo,
by allowing the logs of the walls of the house itself to
extend sufficient distance beyond to make another room,
pen, or division. In this particular case the settler has

put a shed roof of boards upon the division, but the main roof is made of logs in the form of tiles. In Canada these are called *les auges* (pronounced ōge), a name given to them by the French settlers. The back of this house has a steeper roof than the front, which roof, as you see, extends above the ends of *les auges* to keep the rain from beating in at the ends of the wooden troughs. Above the logs on the front side of the small room, pen, or addition the front is covered with shakes. Fig. 240 shows a cabin in the Olympic mountains, but it is only the ordinary American log cabin with a shake roof and no windows. A cooking-stove inside answers for heating apparatus and the stovepipe protrudes above the roof.

The Southern Saddle-Bag or Two-Pen Cabin

Now we come to the most delightful of all forms of a log house. The one shown in Fig. 241 is a very simple one, such as might be built by any group of boys, but I have lived in such houses down South that were very much more elaborate. Frequently they have a second story which extends like the roof over the open gallery between the pens; the chimneys are at the gable ends, that is, on the outside of the house, and since we will have quite a space devoted to fireplaces and chimneys, it is only necessary to say here that in many portions of the South the fireplaces, while broad, are often quite shallow and not nearly so deep as some found in the old houses on Long Island, in New York, and the Eastern States. The open gallery makes a delightful, cool lounging place, also a place for the ladies to sit and sew, and serves as an open-air dining-room during the warm weather; this sort of house is inappropriate and ill fitted for the climate which produced the olebo, the mossback, and the Kanuck, but exactly suited for our Southern States and very pleasant even as far north as Ohio, Indiana, and Illinois. I have lived in one part of every summer for the last twenty-two years in the mountains of northern Pennsylvania. The saddle-bag may be built by boys with the two rooms ten by ten and a gallery six feet wide, or the two rooms six by six and a gallery five feet wide; the plan may be seen on the sketch below the house (Fig. 241).

Where you only expect to use the house in the summer months, a two-pen or saddle-bag can be used with comfort even in the Northern States, but in the winter-time in such States as Michigan and part of New York, the gallery would be filled up with drifting snow.

XXXIX

NATIVE NAMES FOR THE PARTS OF A KANUCK LOG CABIN, AND HOW TO BUILD ONE

IF the writer forgets himself once in a while and uses words not familiar to his boy readers, he hopes they will forgive him and put all such slips down as the result of leaving boys' company once in a while and associating with men. The reader knows that men dearly love big, ungainly words and that just as soon as boys do something worth while the men get busy hunting up some top-heavy name for it.

When one is talking of foreign things, however, it is well to give the foreign names for those things, and, since the next house to be described is not a real American one but a native of Canada, the Canadian names are given for its parts. While in northern Quebec, making notes for the Kanuck, the writer enlisted the interest of a fellow member of the Camp-Fire Club of America, Doctor Alexander Lambert, and through him secured the names of all parts of the Canadian shack.

The author is not a French-Canadian, and, although, like most of his readers, he studied French at school, what he learned of that great language is now securely locked up in one of the safe-deposit vaults of his brain and the key lost.

He owns up to his ignorance because he is a scout and would not try to deceive his readers, also because if the reader's knowledge of French enables him to find some error, the writer can sidestep the mistake and say,

177

"'Tain't mine." But, joking aside, these names are the ones used in the Province of Quebec and are here given not because they are good French but because they are the names used by the builders among the natives known by the Indians as *les habitants*

Local Names of Parts of Cabin

spruce	épinette
balsam	sapin
to chop	boucher, Figs. 113 and 122
to cut	couper
logs	les bois or les billots, *A, A, A,* Figs. 242, 245, also 119, 126, etc.
square	carré
door	porte, Figs. 242, 243
window	châssis, Fig. 243
window-glass	les vitres, 242
the joist on which the floor is laid	les traverses, Fig. 49, *B, B, B, B,* Fig. 244
the floor itself	plancher
the purlins, that is, the two big logs used to support the roof	les poudres, *C, C,* Fig. 244
the roof	couverture, Fig. 242
bark	écorce
birch bark	bouleau
the poles put on a birch-bark roof to keep the bark flat	les péches, Figs. 41, 234, 242
the hollow half-logs sometimes used like tiling on a roof	les auges, Fig. 246
piazza, porch, front stoop, veranda	galerie, Figs. 236, 237, and 241

The only thing that needs explanation is the squaring of the round logs of the cabin. For instance, instead of leaving the logs absolutely round and untouched inside

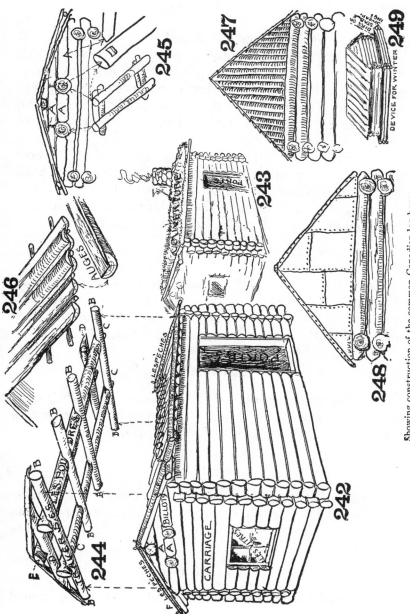

Showing construction of the common Canadian log house.

the camp, after the logs are placed, they are squared off so as to leave a flat surface (Fig. 125). They call this the *carréage*. I do not know whether this is a local name or whether it is an expression peculiar to that Quebec section of Canada or whether it is simply a corruption of better French. It is derived from the word *carrer*, to square.

The perspective drawings (Figs. 242 and 243) show views of the cabin we call the Kanuck. The pen is built exactly as it is built in the houses already described. The windows are placed where the builder desires, as is also the doorway, but when the side-plate logs, that is

Les Traverses

or top side logs, are put in place, then the traverses logs (*B, B, B, B*, Fig. 244) are laid across the pen from one side-plate to the other, their ends resting on top of the side-plates over the traverses logs, the two purlins

Les Poudres

(*C, C*, Fig. 244) are notched and fitted, and over their ends the two pieces *D, D* are fitted, and, resting on the centres of the *D* logs, the ridge log (*E*, Fig. 244) is placed.

Couverture

The roof is made of small logs flattened on the underside or left in their rounded form (Fig. 242) and laid from the ridge logs down, extending over the eaves six or more inches.

Les Péches

The roof logs are then held in place by poles pegged with wooden pegs to the roof (*F, G*, Fig. 242).

Roofing Material

The roof is now covered with a thick layer of browse, hay, straw, dry leaves, or dry grass, and on top of this moist blue clay, yellow clay, hard-pan, or simple mud is spread and trampled down hard, forcing the thatch underneath into all the cracks and crannies and forming a firm covering of clay several inches thick.

Fireplace

The fireplace and chimney may be built inside or outside the cabin, or the house may be heated by a stove and the stovepipe allowed to protrude through a hole in the roof large enough to separate the pipe a safe distance from the wood and straw and amply protected by a piece of sheet iron or tin. Then, after you have stored your *butin* (luggage), you can sit and sing:

> You may pull the *sourdine* out
> You may push the *rabat-joie* in
> But the *boucan* goes up the *cheminée* just the same
> Just the same, just the same,
> But the *boucan* goes up the *cheminée* just the same.

When "l'habitant" hears you sing this verse he will not know what your song is about, but he will slap you on the back, laugh, and call you *Bon Homme chez nous,* but do not get mad at this; it is a compliment and not a bad name.

Clay Roof

A clay roof should be as flat as possible with only pitch enough to shed the water; a shingle roof should have a rise of at least one foot high to four feet wide and a thatched roof should have a rise of 45°, that is, the rise of a line drawn from corner to corner of a square.

Fig. 247 shows a gable filled with upright logs and Fig. 248 shows a tar paper roof and a gable covered with tar paper.

Since Kanucks are cold-climate houses, they frequently have novel means of keeping them warm; one way that I have frequently seen used is to surround them with a log fence shown in Fig. 249, and pack the space between with stable manure or dirt and rotten leaves.

XL

HOW TO MAKE A POLE HOUSE AND HOW TO MAKE A UNIQUE BUT THOROUGHLY AMERICAN TOTEM LOG HOUSE

A POLE house is a log house with the logs set upright. We call it a pole house because, usually, the logs are smaller than those used for a log house. The pole house (Fig. 250) is built in the manner shown by Figs. 171, 172, and 173, but in the present instance the ridge-pole is a log which is allowed to extend some distance beyond the house both in front and rear, and the front end of the ridge-pole is carved in the shape of a grotesque or comical animal's head like those we see on totem-poles. The roof is made of shakes (see Figs. 126 to 130) and the shakes are held in place by poles pegged onto the roof in much the same manner as we have described and called *les pêches* for the Kanuck. This pole cabin may have an old-fashioned Dutch door which will add to its quaintness and may have but one room which will answer the many purposes of a living-room, sleeping-room, and dining-room. A lean-to at the back can be used for a kitchen.

American Totem Log House

But if you really want something unique, build a log house on the general plan shown by Figs. 251 and 252; then carve the ends of all the extending logs to represent the heads of reptiles, beasts, or birds; also carve the posts which support the end logs on the front gallery, porch, or veranda in the form of totem-poles. You may add further

183

to the quaint effect by placing small totem-posts where your steps begin on the walk (Fig. 253) and adding a tall totem-pole (Fig. 255) for your family totem or the totem of your clan. Fig. 252 shows how to arrange and cut your logs for the pens. The dining-room is supposed to be behind the half partition next to the kitchen; the other half of this room being open, with the front room, it makes a large living-room. The stairs lead up to the sleeping-rooms overhead; the latter are made by dividing the space with partitions to suit your convenience.

Before Building

Take your jack-knife and a number of little sticks to represent the logs of your cabin; call an inch a foot or a half inch a foot as will suit your convenience and measure all the sticks on this scale, using inches or parts of inches for feet. Then sit down on the ground or on the floor and experiment in building a toy house or miniature model until you make one which is satisfactory. Next glue the little logs of the pen together; but make the roof so that it may be taken off and put on like the lid to a box; keep your model to use in place of an architect's drawing; the backwoods workmen will understand it better than they will a set of plans and sections on paper. Fig. 251 is a very simple plan and only put here as a suggestion. You can put the kitchen at the back of the house instead of on one side of it or make any changes which suit your fancy; the pen of the house may be ten by twelve or twenty by thirty feet, a camp or a dwelling; the main point is to finish your house up with totems as shown by Fig. 253, and then tell the other fellows where you got the idea.

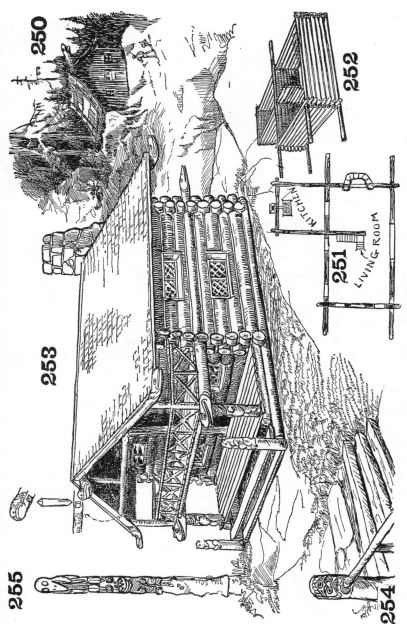

250

252

251 KITCHEN LIVING ROOM

253

255

254

A totem motif. An artistic and novel treatment for a log house.

Peeled Logs

For any structure which is intended to be permanent never use the logs with bark on them; use *peeled* logs. When your house is finished it may look very fresh and new without bark, but one season of exposure to the weather will tone it down so that it will be sufficiently rustic to please your fancy, but if you leave the bark on the logs, a few seasons will rot your house down, making it *too* rustic to suit any one's fancy.

Lay up the pen of this house as already described and illustrated by Figs. 229, 233, etc., and when the sides and front walls have reached the desired height, frame your roof after the manner shown by Fig. 49 or any of the other methods described which may suit your fancy or convenience, but in this case we use the Susitna form for the end plates, which are made by first severing the root of a tree and leaving an elbow or bend at the end of the trunk (Fig. 264). This is flattened by scoring and hewing as is described and illustrated under the heading of the Susitna house. The elbows at the terminals of the end plate are carved to represent grotesque heads (Fig. 253). The house when built is something like the Wyoming olebo (Fig. 236), but with the difference which will appear after careful inspection of the diagram. The Wyoming olebo is a one-story house; this is a two-story house. The Wyoming olebo has a roof built upon a modified plan of a Kanuck; this roof is built on the American log-cabin plan, with the logs continued up to the top of the gable, as are those in the Olympic (Fig. 240). But the present house is supposed to be *very carefully* built; to be sure, it is made of rude material but handled in a very neat and workmanlike manner. Great care must be used in notching and joining the logs, and only the straightest logs which can be had should be used for the walls of the house. The piazza may need some additional supports if there is a wide front to the house, but with a narrow front half, log puncheons will be sufficiently stiff to support themselves.

Totems

The most difficult part about these descriptions, for the writer, is where he attempts to tell you how to make your totems; but remember that a totem, in order to have a *real* totem look, must be very crude and amateurish, a quality that the reader should be able to give it without much instruction. The next important thing is that when you make one side of a head, be it a snake's, a man's, a beast's, or a bird's, make the other side like it. Do not make the head lopsided; make both sides of the same proportions. Flatten the sides of the end of the log enough to give you a smooth surface, then sketch the profile on each side of the log with charcoal or chalk, carve out the head with a chisel, drawing-knife, and jack-knife, and gouge until you have fashioned it into the shape desired. In order to do this the end of the log should be free from the ground and a convenient distance above it. The carving is best done after the house is practically finished; but the two end plates had better be carved before they are hoisted into place.

Totem-Poles

When you carve out the totem-poles (Fig. 256 or 262), the log had better be put on an elongated sawbuck arrangement which will hold it free from the ground and allow one to turn it over as the work may require. Fig. 259 represents a peeled log. On this log one may sketch, with chalk, the various figures here represented, then begin by notching the log (Fig. 258) according to the

notches which are necessary to carve out the totem.
Figs. 260, 261, and 262 show different views of the same
totem figures. Fig. 257 shows how to make a variation
of the totem-pole. Paint your totem heads and figures
red, blue, and yellow, and to suit your fancy; the more
startling they are the better will they imitate the Indian
totems. The weather will eventually tone them down
to the harmonious colors of a Turkish rug.

In "The Boy Pioneers" I have told how to make various other forms of totems, all of which have since been
built by boys and men in different parts of the country.
Mr. Stewart Edward White, a member of the Camp-Fire
Club of America, woodsman, plainsman, mountaineer,
and African hunter and explorer, built himself a totem in
the form of a huge bird twelve feet high from the plans
published in "The Boy Pioneers," and I anticipate no
great difficulty will be encountered by those who try to
totemize a log cabin after the manner shown by Fig. 258.
It will not, however, be a small boy's work, but the small
boys who started at the beginning of this book are older
and more experienced now, and, even if they cannot
handle the big logs themselves, they are perfectly competent to teach their daddies and uncles and their big
brothers how to do it, so they may act as boss builders
and architects and let the older men do the heavy work.
But however you proceed to build this house, when it is
finished you will have a typically native building, and at
the same time different from all others, as quaint as any
bungling bungalow, and in better taste, because it will fit
in the landscape and become part of it and look as if it
belonged there, in place of appearing as if it had been blown
by a tornado from some box factory and deposited in an
unsuitable landscape.

You must understand by this that unsuitable refers
to the fact that a bungalow *does not* belong in the Ameri-

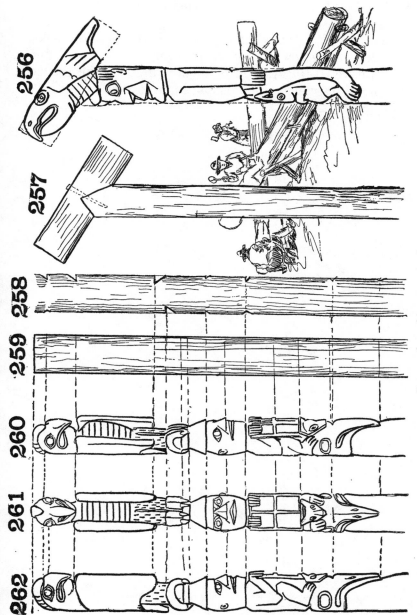

Totem-poles and how to make them.

can landscape, although many of the cottages and shacks, miscalled bungalows, may be thoroughly American and appropriate to the American surroundings despite the exotic name by which some people humble them.

XLI

HOW TO BUILD A SUSITNA LOG CABIN AND HOW TO CUT TREES FOR THE END PLATES

STANDING on a hill overlooking the salt meadows at Hunter's Point, L. I., there was an old farmhouse the roof of which projected over both sides of the house four or five feet. The hill on which it stood has been cut away, the meadows which it overlooked have been filled up with the dirt from the hill, and only a surveyor with his transit and the old property-lines map before him could ever find the former location of this house, but it is somewhere among the tracks of the Long Island Railroad.

Opposite the house, on the other side of the railroad track, in the section known as Dutch Kills of Long Island City, two other houses of the same style of architecture stood; they had double doors—that is, doors which were cut in two half-way up so that you might open the top or bottom half or both halves to suit your fancy. The upper panels of these doors had two drop-lights of glass set in on the bias, and between them, half-way down the upper half, was a great brass knocker with a grip big enough to accommodate both hands in case you really wanted to make a noise.

There was another house of this same description in the outskirts of Hoboken, and I often wondered what the origin of that peculiar roof might be. I found this type of house as far north toward the Hudson Bay as the settlements go, and still farther north the Susitna house explains the origin of the overhanging eaves (Fig. 268).

191

Of course the Susitna, as here drawn, is not exactly the same as that built by the natives on the Susitna River, but the end plates (Fig. 263) are the same as those used in the primitive houses of the Northwest.

How to Cut the Tree

Fig. 264 shows a standing fir-tree and also shows what cuts to make in order to get the right-shaped log for an end plate. Fig. 265 shows the method of scoring and hewing necessary in order to flatten the end of the log as it is in Fig. 266. Fig. 267 shows the style in which the natives roof their Susitnas with logs. The elbows at the end of the plates (Fig. 266) serve to keep the logs of the roof (Fig. 267) from rolling off, but the Susitna log cabin which we are building is expected to have a roof (Fig. 268) of thatch or a roof of shingles, because we have passed the rude shacks, sheds, and shelters used for camps and are now building real houses in which we may live. The Susitna may be built of round logs or of flattened logs (*le carréage*), in which case we can use the General Putnam square notch (Fig. 263) for joining the ends of our logs. In raising the roof, erect the ridge-pole first. The ridge-pole may be set up on two uprights to which it is temporarily nailed, and the upright props may be held in place by the two diagonal props or braces, as shown in Fig. 263. If the logs are squared, cut a small bird's-mouth notch in the rafter where it extends over the side-plate logs of the pen and bevel the top end of your gable rafters to fit against the ridge-pole as in the dia-- grams. The other rafters are now easily put in place, but if the logs are round you must notch the rafters and side-plates as shown by the diagram between Figs. 263 and 267; the dotted lines show where the rafter and the logs come together. Nail your rafters to your ridge-pole

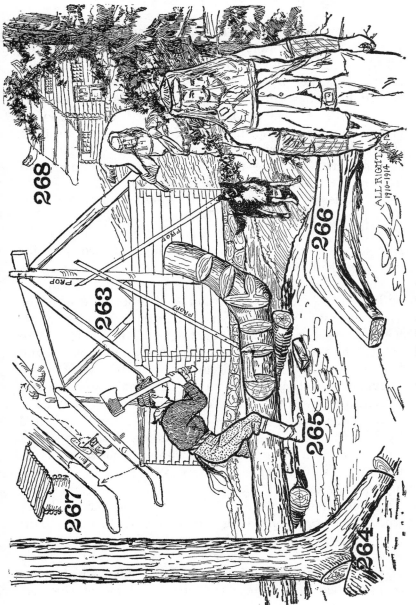

The Susitna log house.

and fasten them to the side-plate with wooden pegs or spikes. The ridge-pole may be allowed to extend, as in Fig. 268, on each side of the cabin or the elbows (Fig. 266) may be attached to each end of the ridge-pole with noses turned up and painted or carved into a fanciful head as in Fig. 268. If the roof is to be shingled, collect a lot of poles about four inches in diameter, flatten them on both sides, and nail them to the rafters not more than two inches apart, allowing the ends of the sticks to extend beyond the walls of the house at least six inches.

If you desire to make your own shingles, saw up a hemlock, pine, or spruce log into billets of one foot four inches long, then with a froe and a mall (Fig. 179) split the shingles from the billets of wood, or use a broadaxe for the same purpose. Broadaxes are dangerous weapons in the hands of an amateur, but the writer split shingles with a broadaxe upon the shores of Lake Erie when he was but seven years old and, as near as he can count he still has ten toes and ten fingers. If you intend to thatch the roof you need not flatten the poles which you fasten across the rafters, because the thatch will hide all unevenness of the underpinning. The poles may be laid at right angles to the rafters between six and eight inches apart and the roof thatched as described and illustrated by Fig. 66. The Susitna form of house is the one from which the old Long Island farmhouses were evolved, although the old Long Islanders copied theirs from the homes they left in Holland, but we must remember that even the effete civilization of Europe once had a back-woods country a long, long time ago, and then they built their houses from the timbers hewn in the forests as our own ancestors did in this country; consequently, many of the characteristics of present-day houses which seem to us useless and unnecessary are survivals of the necessary characteristics of houses made of crude material.

XLII

HOW TO MAKE A FIREPLACE AND CHIMNEY FOR A SIMPLE LOG CABIN

FIG. 269 shows a simple form of fireplace which is practically the granddaddy of all the other fireplaces. It consists of three walls for windbreaks, laid up in stone or sod against some stakes driven in the ground for the purpose of supporting them. The four-cornered stakes are notched or forked and small logs are laid horizontally in these forks and on top of this a pyramidal form of a log pen is built of small logs and billets, and this answers the purpose of a chimney. This style of fireplace is adapted to use in camps and rude shacks like those shown by Figs. 187, 189, 191, and 192; also for the most primitive log cabins, but when we make a real log house we usually plan to have a more elaborate or more finished fireplace and chimney. The ground-plan of Fig. 269 is shown by Fig. 270.

Mud Hearth

Here you see there is a mud hearth, a wall of clay plastered over the stones of the fireplace. This will prevent the fire from cracking and chipping the stones, but clay is not absolutely necessary in this fireplace. When, however, you build the walls of your fireplace of logs and your chimney of sticks the clay *is* necessary to prevent the fire from igniting the woodwork and consuming

it. For a log-framed fireplace, make a large opening in
the wall of your house and against the ends of the logs
where you sawed out the opening, erect jamb pieces of
planks two or three inches thick running up to the log
over the fireplace and spiked to the round ends of the logs
(see plan, Fig. 272). Next, lay your foundation of sill
logs on the fireplace, first two side logs and then a back
log, neatly notched so as to look like the logs in the walls
of the cabin. Build your fireplace walls as shown by
Fig. 271, after which take your mud or clay and make
the hearth by hammering the clay down hard until you
have a firm, smooth foundation. The front hearth may
be made, as shown in the diagram, of stones of any size
from pebbles to flagstones, with the surfaces levelled by
sinking the under-part down into the clay until a uniform level is reached on top. The fireplace may be built
with bricks of moist clay and wet clay used for mortar.
Make the clay walls of the fireplace at least one foot thick
and pack it down hard and tight as you build it. If you
choose you may make a temporary inside wall of plank
as they do when they make cement walls, and then between the temporary board wall and the logs put in your
moist clay and ram it down hard until the top of the
fireplace is reached, after which the boards may be removed and the inside of the fireplace smoothed off by
wiping it with a wet cloth.

Stick Chimney

After the walls of logs and clay are built to top of the
fireplace proper, split some sticks and make them about
one inch wide by one and one half inch thick, or use the
round sticks in the form in which they grow, but peel off
the bark to render them less combustible; then lay them
up as shown by Fig. 261, log-cabin style. With the chim-

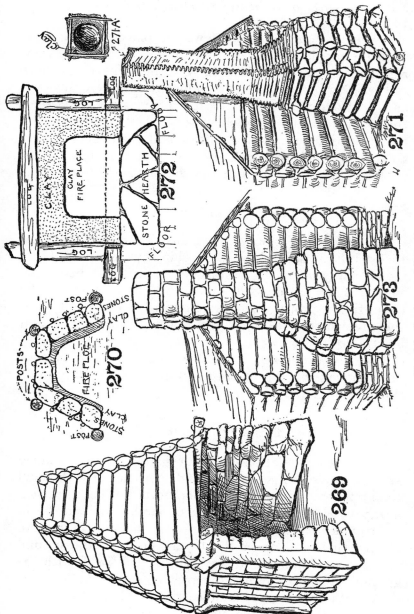

Detail for fireplaces and flues.

ney we have four sides to the wall in place of three sides as in the fireplace. The logs of the fireplace, where they run next to the cabin, may have to be chinked up so as to keep them level, but the chimney should be built level as it has four sides to balance it. Leave a space between the chimney and the outside wall and plaster the sticks thickly with clay upon the outside and much thicker with clay upon the inside, as shown by Fig. 271 *A*, which is supposed to be a section of the chimney.

Durability

All through the mountains of East Tennessee and Kentucky I have seen these stick chimneys, some of them many, many years old. In these mountain countries the fireplaces are lined with stones, but in Illinois, in the olden times, stones were scarce and mud was plenty and the fireplaces were made like those just described and illustrated by Fig. 272.

The stone chimney is an advance and improvement upon the log chimney, but I doubt if it requires any more skill to build.

Chimney Foundation

Dig your foundation for your fireplace and chimney at least three feet deep; then fill the hole up with small cobblestones or broken bluestone until you have reached nearly the level of the ground; upon this you can begin to lay your hearth and chimney foundation. If you fail to dig this foundation the frost will work the ground under your chimney and the chimney will work with the ground, causing it either to upset or to tilt to one side or the other and spoil the looks of your house, even if it does not put your fireplace out of commission.

Stone Chimney

In laying up the stones for your chimney, remember that it makes no difference how rough and uneven it is upon the outside. The more uneven the outside is the more picturesque it will appear, but the smoother and more even the inside is the less will it collect soot and the less will be the danger of chimney fires. Lay your stones in mortar or cement. See that each stone fits firmly in the bed and does not rock and that it breaks joints with the other stone below it. By breaking joints I mean that the crack between the two stones on the upper tier should fit over the middle of the stone on the lower tier; this, with the aid of the cement, locks the stones and prevents any accidental cracks which may open from extending any further than the two stones between which it started. If, however, you do not break joints, a crack might run from the top to the bottom of the chimney causing it to fall apart. Above the fireplace make four walls to your chimney, as you did with your stick chimney (Fig. 271), and let the top of the chimney extend above the roof at least three feet; this will not only help the draught but it will also lessen the danger of fire.

XLIII

HEARTHSTONES AND FIREPLACES

In erecting the fireplace for your cabin the stone work should extend into the cabin itself, thus protecting the ends of the logs from the fire. The stone over the top of the fireplace (*A*, *B*, Fig. 274) rests upon two iron bars; these iron bars are necessary for safety because, although the stone *A*, *B* may bridge the fireplace successfully, the settling of the chimney or the heat of the fire is liable to crack the stone, in which case, unless it is supported by two flat iron bars, it will fall down and wreck your fireplace. The stone *A*, *B* in Fig. 275, has been cracked for fifteen years but, as it rests upon the flat iron bars beneath, the crack does no harm.

In Fig. 274 (the ends of the fireplace) the two wing walls of it are built up inside the cabin to support a plank for a mantelpiece. Another plank *C*, *D* is nailed under the mantelpiece against the log before the stone work is built up. This is only for the purpose of giving a finish to your mantelpiece. The hearth in Fig. 274 is made of odd bits of flat stones laid in cement, but the hearth in Fig. 275 is one big slab of bluestone just as it came from the quarry, and the fireplace in Fig. 275 is lined with firebrick. The two three-legged stools which you see on each side were made by the woodsmen who built the cabin to use in their camp while the cabin was being erected. The stools have occupied the position of honor on each side of the fireplace now for twenty-seven years. The

PLANK

STONE

MANTLE & FIRE—
PLACE

274

275

Fireplace in author's cabin, and suggestion for stone and wood mantel.

mantelpiece in this drawing is made of puncheons with the rounded side out on the two supports and the flat side against the wall; of course, for the mantel itself, the rounded side must be down and the flat side up. This fireplace has been used for cooking purposes and the crane is still hanging over the flames, while up over the mantel you may see, roughly indicated, a wrought-iron broiler, a toaster, and a brazier. The flat shovel hanging to the left of the fireplace is what is known as a "peal," used in olden times to slip under the pies or cakes in the old-fashioned ovens in order to remove them without burning one's fingers.

XLIV

MORE HEARTHS AND FIREPLACES

SOMETIMES it is desired to have a fireplace in the middle of the room. Personally, such a fireplace does not appeal to me, but there are other people who like the novelty of such a fireplace, and Fig. 276 shows one constructed of rough stones. The fireplace is high so that one tending it does not have to stoop and get a backache. The foundation should be built in the ground underneath the cabin and up through the floor. A flat stone covers the top of the fireplace, as in the other drawings. Fig. 277 shows a fireplace with a puncheon support for a plank mantel.

A Plank Mantel

A and B are two half logs, or puncheons, which run from the floor to the ceiling on each side of the fireplace. S, S, S are the logs of the cabin walls. C is the puncheon supporting the mantel and D is the mantel. Fig. 279 shows a section or a view of the mantel looking down on it from the top, a topographical view of it. Fig. 278 is the same sort of a view showing the puncheon A at the other end of the mantel before the mantel is put in place between the two puncheons A and B. In Fig. 279 the reader may see that it will be necessary to cut the corners out of the mantel-board in order to fit it around the puncheons A and B; also, since A and B have rounded

203

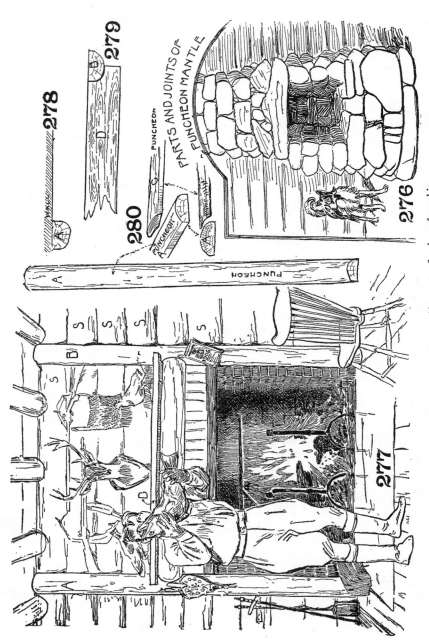

278

279

280

276

PARTS AND JOINTS OF PUNCHEON MANTLE

PUNCHEON

PUNCHEON

PUNCHEON

PUNCHEON

277

Fireplace and mantel of half logs.   Also centre fireplaces for cabin.

surfaces, it will be necessary to so bevel the ends of the puncheon (*C*, Fig. 277) that they will fit on the rounded surfaces of *A* and *B*. Fig. 280 shows the end of *C* bevelled in a perspective view, and also a profile view of it, with the puncheon *A* indicating the manner in which *C* must be cut to fit upon the rounded surface. This makes a simple mantelpiece but a very appropriate one for a log cabin.

XLV

FIREPLACES AND THE ART OF TENDING THE FIRE

ONE of my readers has written to me asking what to do about a fireplace that smokes. Not knowing the fireplace in question, I cannot prescribe for that particular invalid, but I have a long acquaintance with many fireplaces that smoke and fireplaces that do not—in other words, healthy fireplaces with a good digestion and diseased fireplaces functionally wrong with poor digestion—so perhaps the easiest way to answer these questions is to describe a few of my acquaintances among the fireplaces which I have studied.

There is an old fireplace in Small Acres, Binghamton, N. Y., of which I made sketches and took measurements which furnished me data by which I built the fireplaces in my own houses.

In Binghamton fireplaces the side walls are on an angle and converge toward the back of the fireplace, as in Fig. 274. The back also pitches forward, as in Fig. 282. The great advantage of this is the reflecting of more heat into the room.

Fig. 281 shows the fireplace before which I am now working. The fire was started in last November and is now (April 1) still burning, although it has not been rekindled since it was first lighted. This fireplace is well constructed, and on very cold days I have the fire burning out on the hearth fully a foot beyond the line of the mantel without any smoke coming into my studio.

Fig. 282 shows a diagram with the dimensions of my

206

studio fireplace and represents the vertical section of it. I give these for the benefit of the people who want to know how to build a fireplace which will not smoke. But, of course, even the best of fireplaces will smoke if the fire is not properly arranged. With smoke the angle of reflection would be equal to the angle of incidence did not the constant tendency of smoke to ascend modify this rule.

Throw a rubber ball against the wall and the direction from your hand to where it strikes the wall makes the angle of incidence; when the ball bounces away from the wall it makes the angle of reflection.

Management of the Fire

But, before we enter into the question regarding the structure of the flue we will take up the management of the fire itself. In the first place, there is but one person who can manage a fire, and that is yourself. Servants never did and never will learn the art, and, as I am writing for men, and the ladies are not supposed to read this article, I will state that the fair sex show a like deficiency in this line. The first thing a woman wants to do with a fire is to make the logs roost on the andirons, the next thing is to remove every speck of ashes from the hearth, and then she wonders why the fire won't burn.

The ashes have not been removed from my studio fire since it was first lighted last fall. Ashes are absolutely essential to control a wood-fire and to keep the embers burning overnight. Fig. 288 shows the present state of the ashes in my studio fire. You will see by this diagram that the logs are not resting on the andirons. I only use the andirons as a safeguard to keep the logs from rolling out on the hearth. If the fire has been replenished late in the evening with a fresh log, before retiring I pull the front or the ornamental parts of the andirons to the hearth and then lay the shovel and poker across them horizontally. When the burning log is covered with ashes and the andirons arranged in this manner you can retire at night with a feeling of security and the knowledge that if your house catches afire it will not be caused by the embers in your fireplace. Then in the morning all you have to do is to shovel out the ashes from the rear of the fireplace, put in a new backlog, and bed it in with ashes, as shown in Fig. 286. Put your glowing embers next to the backlog and your fresh wood on top of that and sit down to your breakfast with the certainty that your fire will be blazing before you get up from the table.

Don't make the mistake of poking a wood-fire, with the idea, by that means, of making it burn more briskly, or boosting up the logs to get a draught under them.

Two logs placed edge to edge, like those in Fig. 288, with hot coals between them, will make their own draught, which comes in at each end of the log, and, what is essential in fire building, they keep the heat between themselves, constantly increasing it by reflecting it back from one to the other. If you happen to be in great haste to make the flames start, don't disturb the logs but use a pair of bellows.

Fig. 287 shows a set of the logs which will make the best-constructed fireplace smoke. The arrow-point shows the line of incidence or the natural direction which the smoke would take did not the heat carry it upward.

Fig. 285 shows the same logs arranged so that the angle of incidence strikes the back of the chimney and the smoke ascends in the full and orderly manner. But both Figs. 285 and 287 are clumsily arranged. The *B* logs in each case should be the backlog and the small logs *A* and *C* should be in front of *B*.

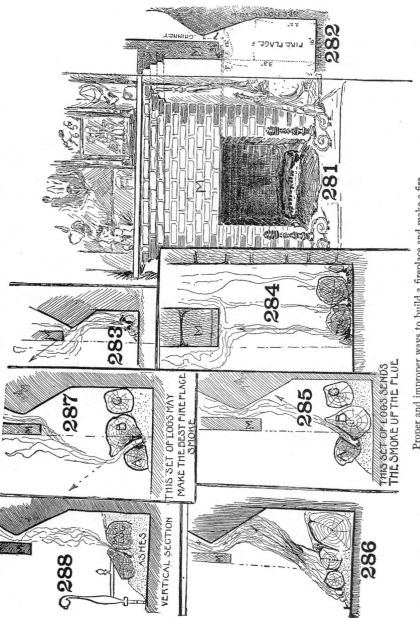

Proper and improper ways to build a fireplace and make a fire.

In all of the fireplaces which we have described you will note that the top front of the fireplace under the mantel extends down several inches below the angle of the chimney.

Fig. 283 shows a fireplace that is improperly built. This is from a fireplace in a palatial residence in New York City, enclosed in an antique Italian marble mantel, yellow with age, which cost a small fortune. The fireplace was designed and built by a firm of the best architects, composed of men famed throughout the whole of the United States and Europe, *but the fireplace smoked* because the angle of the chimney was below the opening of the fireplace and, consequently, sent the smoke out into the room. This had to be remedied by setting a piece of thick plate glass over the top of the fireplace, thus making the opening smaller and extending it below the angle of the chimney.

Fig. 284 shows the most primitive form of fireplace and chimney. One that a child may see will smoke unless the fire is kept in the extreme back of the hearth.

The advantages of ashes in your fireplace are manifold. They retain the heat, keep the hot coals glowing overnight, and when the fire is too hot may be used to cover the logs and subdue the heat. But, of course, if you want a clean hearthstone and the logs roosting upon the andirons, and are devoid of all the camp-fire sentiment, have some asbestos gas-logs. There will be no dust or dirt, no covering up at night with ashes, no bill for cord-wood, and it will look as stiff and prim as any New England old maid and be as devoid of sentiment and art as a department-store bargain picture frame.

XLVI

THE BUILDING OF THE LOG HOUSE

How a Forty-Foot-Front, Two-Story Pioneer Log House
Was Put Up with the Help of "Backwoods Farmers"
—Making Plans with a Pocket Knife.

OUR log house on the shore of Big Tink Pond, Pike
County, Pa., was built long before the general public
had been educated to enjoy the subtle charms of wild
nature, at a time when nature-study was confined to scientists and children, and long before it was fashionable to
have wild fowl on one's lawn and wild flowers in one's
garden. At that time only a few unconventional souls
spent their vacations out of sight of summer hotels,
camping on the mountain or forest trails. The present
state of the public mind in regard to outdoor life has
only been developed within the last few years, and when
I first announced my intention of hunting up some accessible wild corner and there erecting a log house for a
summer studio and home I found only unsympathetic
listeners. But I was young and rash at that time, and
without any previous experience in building or the aid
of books to guide me and with only such help as I could
find among backwoods farmers I built a forty-foot-front,
two-story log house that is probably the pioneer among
log houses erected by city men for summer homes. It
gave Mr. Charles Wingate the suggestions from which he
evolved Twilight Park in the Catskills. Twilight Park,

being the resort of literary people and their friends, did much to popularize log houses with city people.

The deserted farms of New England offer charming possibilities for those whose taste is for nature with a shave, hair cut, and store clothes, but for lovers of un-tamed nature the waste lands offer stronger inducements for summer-vacation days, and there is no building which fits so naturally in a wild landscape as a good, old-fashioned log cabin. It looks as if it really belonged there and not like a windfall from some passing whirlwind.

When I make the claim that any ordinary man can build himself a summer home, I do not mean to say that he will not make blunders and plenty of them; only fools never make mistakes, wise men profit by them, and the reader may profit by mine, for there is no lack of them in our log house at Big Tink. But the house still stands on the bank overlooking the lake and is practically as sound as it was when the last spike was driven, twenty-seven years ago.

Almost all of the original log cabins that were once sprinkled through the eastern part of our country disappeared with the advent of the saw-mill and the few which still exist in the northern part of the country east of the Alleghany Mountains would not be recognized as log houses by the casual observer, for the picturesque log exteriors have been concealed by a covering of clapboards.

To my surprise I discovered that even among the old mountaineers I could find none who had ever attended a log-rolling frolic or participated in the erection of a real log house. Most of these old fellows, however, could remember living in such houses in their youth, but they could not understand why any sane man of to-day wanted "to waste so much good lumber," and in the quaint old American dialect still preserved in these regions they

Wildlands, the author's log house in Pike County, Pa.

explained the wastefulness of my plans and pointed out to me the number of good planks which might be sawed from each log.

Fig. 290, *B*, shows the plans of the house, which will be seen to be a modification of the Southern "saddle-bag" cabin—two houses under one roof. By referring to Fig. 289 it will be seen that above the gallery there is a portico, which we called the "afterthought" because it did not appear upon the original plans. We got the hint, as "Jimmy" called it, when it was noticed that chance had ordained that the two "*A*" logs should protrude much farther than the others. "Don't saw them off," I exclaimed; "we will have a balcony"; and so the two "*A*" logs were left, and this gave us room for a balcony over the gallery, back of which is a ten-by-ten bedroom, while the two large bedrooms on each side have doors opening on the six-foot passageway, which is made still broader by the addition of the balcony.

It will be seen that there is a stairway marked out on the ground plan, but there was none on the original plan, for, to tell the honest truth, I did not know where to put the stairs until the logs were in place. However, it is just such problems that lend charm to the work of building your own house. An architect or a professional builder would have the thing all cut and dried beforehand and leave nothing to chance and inspiration; this takes the whole charm out of the work when one is building for recreation and the pleasure to be derived from the occupation.

When our house was finished we had no shutters to the windows and no way of closing up the open ends of the gallery, and my helpers told me that I must not leave the house that way because stray cattle would use the house for a stable and break the windows with their horns as they swung their heads to drive away the flies. So we

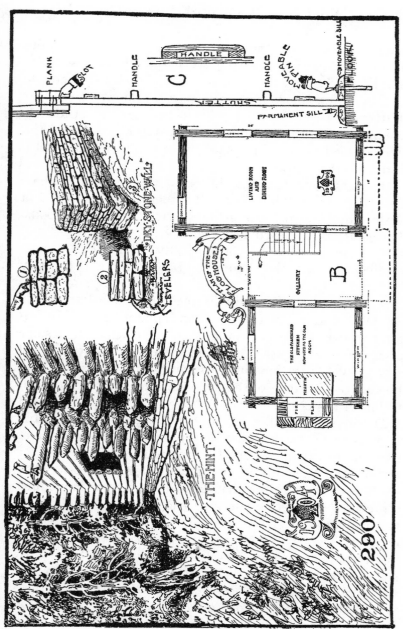

Details of author's log house, Wildlands.

290

nailed boards over these openings when we closed the house for the winter.   Later we invented some shutters (see *C*, Fig. 290) which can be put up with little trouble and in a few moments.   Fig. 290, *C*, shows how these shutters are put in place and locked on the inside by a movable sill that is slid up against the bottom of the shutters and fastened in place by iron pins let into holes bored for the purpose.

Of course, this forms no bar to a professional burglar, but there is nothing inside to tempt cracksmen, and these professional men seldom stray into the woods. The shutters serve to keep out cattle, small boys, and stray fishermen whose idle curiosity might tempt them to meddle with the contents of a house less securely fastened.

A house is never really finished until one loses interest in it and stops tinkering and planning homely improvements.   This sort of work is a healthy, wholesome occupation and just the kind necessary to people of sedentary occupations or those whose misfortune it is to be engaged in some of the nerve-racking business peculiar to life in big cities.

Dwellers in our big cities do not seem to realize that there is any other life possible for them than a continuous nightmare existence amid monstrous buildings, noisy traffic, and the tainted air of unsanitary streets.   They seem to have forgotten that the same sun that in summer scorches the towering masonry and paved sidewalks until the canyon-like streets become unbearable also shines on green woods, tumbling waters, and mirror-like lakes; or, if they are dimly conscious of this fact, they think such places are so far distant as to be practically out of their reach in every sense.   Yet in reality the wilderness is almost knocking at our doors, for within one hundred miles of New York bears, spotted wildcats, and timid deer live unconfined in their primitive wild condition. Fish caught in the streams can be cooked for dinner in New York the same day.

In 1887, when the writer was himself a bachelor, he went out into the wilderness on the shores of Big Tink Pond, upon which he built the log house shown in the sketch. At first he kept bachelor hall there with some choice spirits, not the kind you find in bottles on the barroom shelf, but the human kind who love the outdoor world and nature, or he took his parents and near relatives with him for a vacation in the woods. Like all sensible men, in course of time he married, and then he took his bride out to the cabin in the woods. At length the time came when he found it necessary to shoulder his axe and go to the woods to secure material for a new *piece of furniture.* He cut the young chestnut-trees, peeled them, and with them constructed a crib; and every year for the last eight years that crib has been occupied part of the season. Thus, you see, a camp of this kind becomes hallowed with the most sacred of human memories and becomes a joy not only to the builder thereof but also to the coming generation. At the big, open fire in the grill-room, with the old-fashioned cooking utensils gathered from farmhouses on Long Island, I have cooked venison steaks, tenderloin of the great northern hare, the plump, white breasts of the ruffed grouse, all broiled over the hot coals with slices of bacon, and when done to a turn, placed in a big platter with fresh butter and served to a crowd who watched the operation and sniffed the delicious odor until they literally drooled at the corners of their mouths. As the house was built on a deer runway, all these things were products of the surrounding country, and on several occasions they have all been served at one meal.

XLVII

HOW TO LAY A TAR PAPER, BIRCH BARK, OR PATENT ROOFING

Preparing the Roofing for Laying

BIRCH BARK and patent roofing are more pliable than tin or shingles, consequently taking less time to lay and making it easier work. In very cold weather put your patent roofing in a warm room a few hours before using it. Never try to cut birch bark, tar paper, or patent roofing with a dull knife.

Roofing Foundation

No matter what sort of roofing material is used, do not forget the great importance of the roofing foundation (Figs. 296 and 298). If the foundation is poor or uneven the roofing will be poor and uneven, even if only the best roofing material is used. The sheathing boards should be matched if possible and of uniform thickness, laid close, and free from nails, protruding knots, and sharp edges. Do not use green lumber; the sun is almost certain to shrink and warp it. Sometimes it will even break the roofing material. On very particular work, where the rafters are wide apart, the best builders recommend laying a course of boards over the planking at right angles to it.

Valleys

If there are valleys in the roof (Fig. 298) use a long strip of roofing and lay it up and down in the direction of the valleys. Press the strip into the hollow so that it takes the shape of the valley itself. Allow the edges of the roofing to overlap the strip in the valley an equal distance on both sides of the valley (Fig. 298).

How to Lay the Roofing

Begin at the eaves to lay the roofing (Fig. 299). Always lay the roll of patent roofing with the inside surface to the weather and in the same direction that the boards run—not at right angles to them. Begin nailing at the centre of the edges of the strips and work both ways to the ends—never the reverse, as the roofing may become wrinkled, twisted, or crooked. Always set caps even with the edge of the laps about two inches apart between their centres.

Gutters

To finish gutters, fasten and carefully cement with the pitch or tar or prepared composition the edge of the strip about half-way to the gutter. Bring the other edge onto the roof, then lay the next strip over this strip so that it will overlap at least two inches. Proceed to lay the balance of the roofing in the same way. Never nail the middle of the strips; nail only along the edges. The end strips should always be lapped over the edges of the roof and fastened (Figs. 297 and 299).

Before fastening laps paint a two-inch strip with the tar or pitch cement which comes with all patent roofing in order to stick it to the lower strip of roofing and to make a tight joint when put in place.

Do not drive nails carelessly or with too much force and be sure the cap fits snugly against the roofing. If nails go into holes or open cracks, do not remove them but thoroughly cement around them. Allow six inches for overlaps for joints where one strip joins another (Fig. 299, *B*). Be sure that two strips of roofing never meet at the ridge leaving a joint to invite a leak over the ridge-pole. Examine the diagrams if you fail to understand the description.

How to Patch a Shingle Roof

The reader must not suppose that the roof of my camp was made of flannel because it shrank, for the whole house, which was made of logs, diminished in size as the wood became seasoned; so that now each log averages a quarter of an inch less in width than it did when the house was built twenty odd years ago. There are just one hundred logs in the house, which makes the house twenty-five inches smaller than it was when it was built, but I cannot point out the exact spot where the two feet and one inch are missing. Neither do I know that this had anything to do with the opening in the roof about the chimney; but I do know that the opening gradually became wider and wider until it not only admitted the entrance of numerous flying squirrels and other varmints but also let in the rain and snow and consequently it had to be remedied. Neither the flying squirrels nor the elements can now enter at that point.

The Connecticut Yankees stop the leaks around the big chimneys of the old farmhouses with mortar or concrete, but at permanent camps cement is not always handy, and even if one is living in a farmhouse it will probably necessitate quite a long drive to procure it. If, however, there happens to be on hand some strips of the various

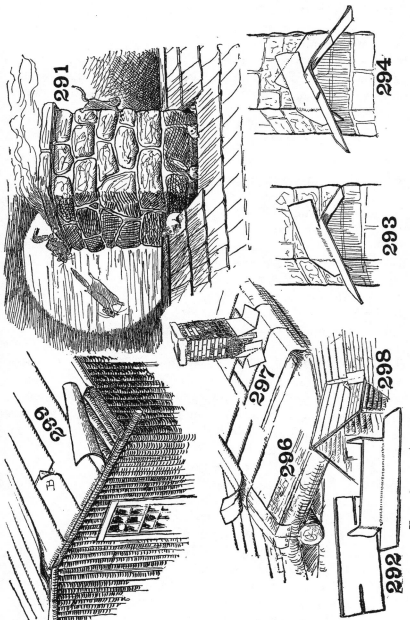

How to lay a composition roof and how to cover space around flue. (Fig. 295 is on next plate.)

tar roofing compounds, some old tin, or even a good piece of oilcloth—by which I mean a piece that may be so worn as to have been cast aside and yet not so perforated with holes that it will admit the rain—it may be used to stop the leak.

Fixtures for Applying Roofing

The complete roofing kit consists of cement, caps, and nails. The galvanized caps and nails are the best to use; they won't rust. Square caps have more binding surface than the ordinary round ones; but we can mend "with any old thing."

Fig. 291 shows a chimney from which the roof of the house is parted, leaving a good-sized opening around the smoke-stack. To cover this, take a piece of roofing compound, tin, oilcloth, tar paper, or paroid and cut as is shown in the upper diagram (Fig. 292). Make the slits in the two ends of the material of such a length that when the upper ends are bent back, as in the lower diagram (Fig. 292), they will fit snugly around the chimney. You will need one piece like this for each side of the chimney. Where the ends of the chimney butt against the ridge of the roof you will require pieces slit in the same manner as the first but *bent differently*. The upper lobe in this case is bent on the bias to fit the chimney, while the lower one is bent over the ridge of the roof (Figs. 293 and 294).

To better illustrate how this is done, Fig. 293 is supposed to show the chimney with the roof removed. Fig. 294 is the same view of the chimney with the two pieces in place. You will need four pieces, two at each end of the chimney, to cover the ridge of the roof.

With all the many varieties of tar paper and composition roofing there come tacks or wire nails supplied with round tin disks perforated in the centre, which are used as washers to prevent the nail from pulling through the roofing.

Fig. 295 shows the chimney with the patches around it tacked in place, and the protruding ends of the parts trimmed off according to the dotted lines. Fig. 297 shows the way the roofing people put flashing on; but I like my own way, as illustrated by Figs. 291, 292, 293, 294, and 295. It must not be taken for granted that every camp or farmhouse has a supply of tin washers, but we know that every camp and farmhouse does have a supply of tin cans, and the washers may be made from these, as shown by Figs. 300 and 301. Knock the cans apart at their seams and cut the tin up into pieces like the rectangular one shown under the hand in Fig. 301. Bend these pieces in their centres so as to make them into squares, then place them on a piece of soft wood and punch holes in them by driving a wire nail through the tin and you will have better washers than those you can buy although they may not be so handsome.

Patched Roofs and New Shingles

Any decent shingled roof should last fifteen years without repairing and many of them last nearly twice that time. But there comes a time when the roof begins to leak and needs mending; when that time comes, with your jack-knife whittle a number of little wooden pegs or splints each about six inches long and a little thicker than a pipe-stem with which to

Mark the Holes

Go up in the attic and wherever you see daylight through the roof push through the hole a wooden peg to mark the spot. Then, when you have finished and are ready to climb on the roof, take off your shoes, put on a pair of woollen socks, and there will be little danger of your slipping. New india rubber shoes with corrugated soles are also good to wear when climbing on the roof.

In Fig. 295½ you will see two of the pegs sticking through the roof marking the holes, and below is a larger view of one of these pegs connected with the upper ones by dotted lines.

Sheet-Iron Shingles

To mend simple cracks or holes like these it is only necessary to bend up bits of tin or sheet iron (Fig. 300) and drive the metal shingle up underneath the shingle above the hole so that the "weather" part of the tin covers the leak, or drive it under the leaking shingle itself, or drive a new shingle up under or over the damaged one. Where there is a bad place in the roof it may be necessary to make a patch of a number of shingles like the one shown in the right-hand corner of Fig. 295½, but even then it is not necessary to remove the old shingles unless the hole is very large.

These patches of old tin or new shingles do not look handsome on an old roof, but they serve their purpose in keeping out the rain and snow and preventing moisture from rotting the timbers. The weather will soon tone down the color of the new shingles so that they will not be noticeable and you will have the satisfaction of having a dry roof over your head. There is only one thing worse than a leaky roof and that is a leaky boat.

Practical Patching

In these days when everybody with a few hundred dollars in pocket is very sensibly using it to buy a farm and farmhouse so as to be able for a part of the year to

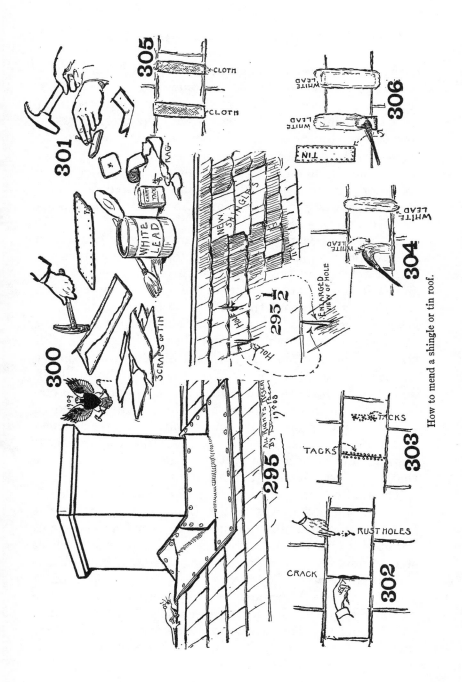

How to mend a shingle or tin roof.

return to the simple life of our ancestors it is very necessary that we should also know something of the simple economies of those days, for when one finds oneself out on a farm there is no plumber around the corner and no tinsmith on the next block whom one may call upon to repair breaks and the damage done by time and weather on an old farmhouse. The ordinary man under these conditions is helpless, but some are inspired by novel ideas, as, for instance, the man who mended the leaking roof with porous plasters.

But for the benefit of those who are not supplied with a stock of porous plasters I will tell how to do the plumbing and how to mend the tin roof with old bits of tin, rags, and white lead; and to begin with I want to impress upon the reader's mind that this will be no bungling, unsightly piece of work, but much more durable and just as neat as any piece of work which the professionals would do for him. In the first place, if you have an old tin roof on one of the extensions of your house or on your house itself, do not be in haste to replace it with a new one. Remember that most of the modern sheet tin is made by modern methods and its life is not an extended one. The sheet *steel* they often use in place of sheet *iron* rapidly disintegrates and such a roof will not last you half the time that a properly patched old one will.

The roof of the house in which I am writing this article is made of tin and was made about sixty years ago; it has been patched and mended but to no great extent, and it bids fair to outlive me. Had it been made of sheet steel it would have been necessary to renew it many times since that period. So, if you find that the tin roof to your farmhouse, bungalow, or camp leaks in consequence of some splits at the seams and a few rust holes patch them yourself. Fig. 301 shows the only material necessary for that purpose. You do not even need a pair of shears to cut your tin, for it is much better folded over and hammered into shape, as shown by Fig. 301. Fig. 302 shows a crack and some rust holes in the tin roof. Take your carpet-tacks and hammer and neatly tack down the edges of the opening, as shown by Fig. 303. If there is any difficulty in driving tacks through the tin roof, use a small wire nail and hammer to first punch the holes. Put the tacks close together. With your paint-brush thickly coat the mended parts with white lead, as shown by Fig. 304. Cut a strip of a rag to fit over the holes and tack it at its four corners, as shown by Fig. 305. Now, then, cover the rag with a thick coat (Fig. 306) of the white lead. Next tack the tin over the wounded spots, putting the tacks close together, as shown by Fig. 306. Afterward coat the tin with a covering of white lead and the patchwork is done. The roof will not leak again at those spots in the next twenty years. This will leave white, unsightly blotches on the roof, but after the white lead is dry a few dabs with the red roof paint will make the white patches the same color as the surrounding tin and effectually conceal them.

Do not forget the importance of carefully going over your roof after it is mended and make sure that every joint is properly covered, tacked, and thoroughly coated with white lead. Cover all joints, nails, and caps with a coat of white lead. Water will not run through the tin roofing, but it will find its way through nail holes, rust holes, and open seams if they are not made absolutely tight.

Plumbing

After I had finished doctoring up the kitchen roof of my farmhouse, I discovered that the drain-pipe from the kitchen sink had a nasty leak where the pipe ran through the cellar. Of course, there was no plumber handy—plumbers do not live in farming districts—so it was "up to" me and my helper to stop the leak as best we could. A few blows on the lead with the hammer, carefully administered, almost closed the hole. I then had recourse to the white lead which I had been using on the kitchen roof, and I daubed the pipe with paint; still the water oozed through; but after I had applied a strip of linen to the leak and then neatly wrapped it round and painted the whole of it with white lead the leak was effectually stopped, and the pipe is apparently as good now, six years after the mending, as it was when it was new.

In this sort of work it must be remembered that it is the white lead we depend upon, and the other material which we use—the tin and the rags—are only for the purpose of protecting and holding the white lead in place. Of course, a roof may be mended with tar, but that is always unsightly and insists upon running when heated by a hot sun; besides, it is most difficult to conceal and does not come ready for use like white lead.

If the leak happens to be around the chimney it can be mended by bending pieces of tin up against the chimney according to the diagram shown for the tar paper and patent roofings (Figs. 295 and 297).

Flashings, Chimneys, Walls, Etc.

Lead or copper is best for flashings, but in case metal is not convenient you will find that various patent roofing materials are good substitutes. Run the strips of roofing to the angle formed by the object to be flashed and extend the same up the object three or four inches. Fasten these strips to the roof in the usual way or by nailing cleats of wood over the top edges.

Leaks in tubs, barrels, and tanks used about the farm

can be mended with rags, tin, and white lead in the manner described for the roof and pipe. Also leaks in the leaders running from the roof may be treated in the same manner, but if you must get new leaders for your house by no means replace the old ones with *galvanized-steel* tubes. You can tell the difference between galvanized steel and galvanized iron by its appearance. The steel is brighter and more silvery than the iron, but my experience is that the steel will last only two or three years; sometimes one season puts steel pipes out of commission, whereas galvanized iron will last indefinitely. After having three sets of galvanized-steel leaders on my town house, I had them replaced with copper leaders; for, although the expense is greater, I have found it more economical in the end. For people having plenty of money to spend on their country houses I would advise the use of copper leaders, but folks of limited means will save money patching up the old tin ones or old galvanized ones instead of replacing them with galvanized steel, which is of little service for outdoor wear. There are, I believe, only a few firms who now manufacture galvanized iron, but your architect can find them if you insist upon it.

XLVIII

HOW TO MAKE A CONCEALED LOG CABIN INSIDE OF A MODERN HOUSE

IT was because the writer knew that a great many men and all the boys rebelled against the conventionalities and restrictions of a modern house that he first invented and suggested the surprise den and told how to make one years ago in the *Outing* magazine. Since that article appeared the idea has been adopted by a numer of people. There is a beautiful one in Toledo, O., where the writer was entertained during the floods, and Doctor Root, of Hartford, Conn., has even a better one in his home in that Yankee city. Fig. 308 shows a rough sketch of a corner of Doctor Root's surprise den which he calls his "loggery."

From the outside of the house there is no indication of anything upon the inside that may not be found in any conventional dwelling, which is the proper way to build the surprise den.

Figs. 307, 309, and 310 are sketches made as suggestions to those wishing to add the surprise den to their dwelling.

To fathers and mothers having sons anywhere from twelve to thirty years of age, it is almost a necessity nowadays to give these boys a room of their own, popularly known as the "den," a retreat where they can go and sit in a chair without having fancy embroidered tidies adhere to their coat collars, where they can lean back in their chairs, if they choose, with no danger of ruining the valu-

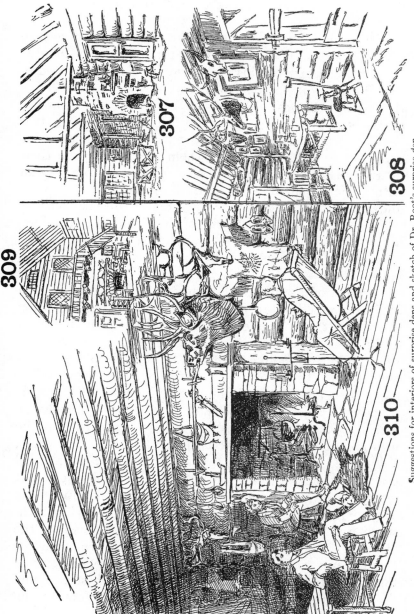

Suggestions for interiors of surprise dens and sketch of Dr. Root's surprise den.

able Hepplewhite or breaking the claw feet off a rare Chippendale—a place where they can relax.   The greater the contrast between this room and the rest of the house, the greater will be the enjoyment derived by the boys to whom it belongs.   The only two surprise dens which I have personally visited are the pride of the lives of two gentlemen who are both long past the years generally accorded to youth, but both of them are still boys in their hearts.   The truth is a surprise den appeals to any man with romance in his soul; and the more grand, stately, and formal his house may be, the greater will the contrast be and the greater the surprise of this den.   It is a unique idea and makes a delightful smoking-room for the gentlemen of the house as well as a den for the boys of the house.

If the reader's house is already built, the surprise den may be erected as an addition; it may be built as a log cabin after the manner of any of those previously described in this book, or it may be made an imitation log cabin by using slabs and nailing them on the walls in place of real whole logs.   Doctor Root's surprise den, or "loggery," is made of whole logs and chinked with moss.   Fig. 310 is supposed to be made of slabs, half logs, or puncheons nailed to the walls and ceiling and so arranged that the visitor cannot detect the deception.   Personally, however, I do not like deception of any sort and would recommend that the house be made, if possible, of whole logs; but whatever way you build it, remember that it must have a generous, wide fireplace, a crane, and a good hearthstone, and that your furniture must either be made of the material to be found in the woods or selected from the antique furniture of some old farmhouse, not mahogany furniture, but Windsor chairs, three-legged stools, and deal-wood tables—such furniture as might be found in an old pioneer's home.

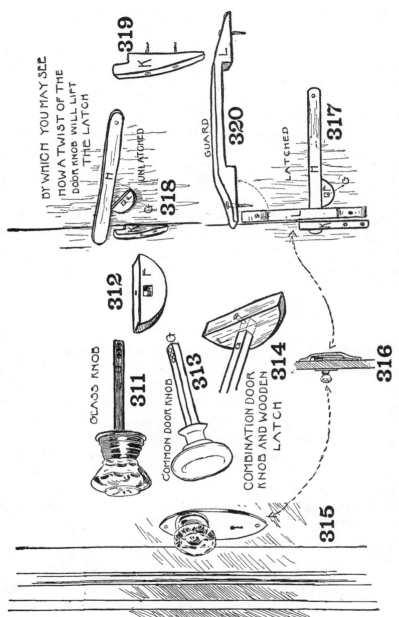

BY WHICH YOU MAY SEE HOW A TWIST OF THE DOOR KNOB WILL LIFT THE LATCH

UNLATCHED

318

319

K

GUARD

320

LATCHED

317

GLASS KNOB

311

312

COMMON DOOR KNOB

313

COMBINATION DOOR KNOB AND WOODEN LATCH

314

316

315

Details of combined door-knob and wooden latch.

The principal thing to the surprise den, however, is the doorway. The outside of the door—that is, the side seen from the main part of the house—should be as formal as its surroundings and give no indication of what might be on the other side. If it opens from the most formal room in the house, so much the better. Fig. 321 shows the outside of the door of the surprise den; I do not mean by this outside of the house but a doorway facing the dining-room, library, drawing-room, or parlor. Fig. 321 shows one side of the door and Fig. 322 the other side of the same door. In this instance one side of the door is supposed to have a bronze escutcheon and a glass knob (Figs. 315 and 316). Of course, any other sort of a knob (Fig. 313) will answer our purpose, but the inside, or the surprise-den side, of the door must have

A Wooden Latch

After some experiments I discovered that this could be easily arranged by cutting a half-round piece of hardwood (*F*, Fig. 312) to fit upon the square end *G* of the knob (Figs. 311 and 313) and be held in place with a small screw (Fig. 314). When this arrangement is made for the door and the knob put in place as it is in Figs. 315 and 316, a simple wooden latch (Fig. 317) with the catch *K* (Fig. 319) and the guard (Fig. 320) may be fastened upon the den side of the door as shown by *K*, *L*, (Fig. 317). When the door is latched the wooden piece *F* fits underneath the latch as shown by Fig. 317. When the knob is turned, it turns the half disk and lifts the latch *H* as shown in Fig. 318; this, of course, opens the door, and the visitor is struck with amazement upon being ushered into a pioneer backwoods log cabin, where after-dinner coffee may be served, where the gentlemen may retire to smoke their cigars, where the master of the house may retire,

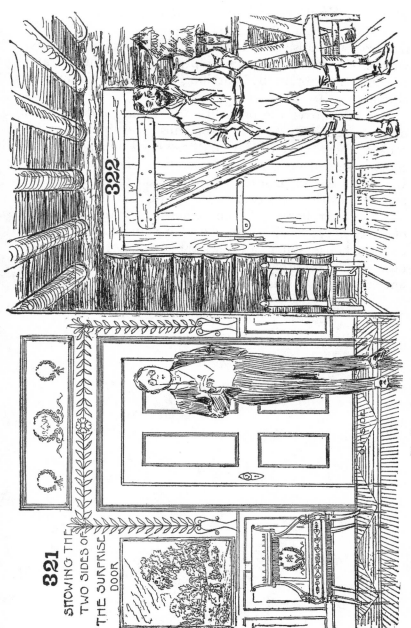

The "surprise den." A log house inside a modern mansion.

free from the noise of the children, to go over his accounts, write his private letters, or simply sit before the fire and rest his tired brain by watching the smoke go up the chimney.

Here also, over the open fire, fish, game, and chickens may be cooked, as our grandams and granddaddies cooked them, and quaint, old-fashioned luncheons and suppers served on earthenware or tin dishes, camp style. In truth, the surprise den possesses so many charming possibilities that it is destined to be an adjunct to almost every modern home. It can be enclosed within the walls of a city house, a suburban house, or added as a wing to a country house, but in all cases the outside of the surprise den should conform in material used and general appearance to the rest of the house so as not to betray the secret.

XLIX

HOW TO BUILD APPROPRIATE GATEWAYS FOR GROUNDS ENCLOSING LOG HOUSES, GAME PRE-SERVES, RANCHES, BIG COUNTRY ESTATES, AND LAST BUT NOT LEAST BOY SCOUTS' CAMP GROUNDS

THE great danger with rustic work is the temptation, to which most builders yield, to make it too fancy and intricate in place of practical and simple. Figs. 323, 324, 325, and 326 are as ornamental as one can make them without incurring the danger of being overdone, too ornate, too fancy to be really appropriate.

Which Would You Rather Do or Go Fishing?

Fig. 328 is a gate made of upright logs with bevelled tops protected by plank acting as a roof, and a flattened log fitting across the top. The gate and fence, you may see, are of simple construction; horizontal logs for the lower part keep out small animals, upright posts and rails for the upper part keep out larger animals and at the same time do not shut out the view from the outside or the inside of the enclosure. Fig. 324 shows a roof gateway designed and made for the purpose of supplying building sites for barn swallows or other useful birds. The fence for this one is a different arrangement of logs, practical and not too fancy. Fig. 325 shows a modification of the gate shown by Fig. 323; in this one,

237

323   324   325   326

Which would you rather do or go fishing?   Suggestions for log gates.

however, in place of a plank protecting bevelled edges of the upright logs, two flattened logs are spiked on like rafters to a roof, the apex being surmounted by a bird-house. Fig. 326 shows another gateway composed of two upright logs with a cross log overhead in which holes have been excavated for the use of white-breasted swallows, bluebirds, woodpeckers, or flickers. Fig. 327 is another simple but picturesque form of gateway, where the cross log at the top has its two ends carved after the fashion of totem-poles. In place of a wooden fence a stone wall is shown. The ends of the logs (Fig. 327), which are embedded in the earth, should first be treated with two or three coats of creosote to prevent decay; but since it is the moisture of the ground that causes the decay, if you arrange your gate-posts like those shown in the vertical section (Fig. 328), they will last practically forever. Note that the short gate-post rests upon several small stones with air spaces between them, and pointed ends of the upright logs rest upon one big stone. The gate-post is fastened to the logs by crosspieces of board running horizontally from log to the post, and these are enclosed inside the stone pier so that they are concealed from view. This arrangement allows all the water to drain from the wood, leaving it dry and thus preventing decay. Fig. 329 shows another form of gate-post of more elaborate structure, surmounted by the forked trunk of a tree; these parts are supposed to be spiked together or secured in place by hardwood pegs.

Never forget to add the bird-house or bird shelter to every gateway you make; it is more important than the gate itself. In my other books I have described and told how to make various forms of bird-houses, including my invention of the woodpecker's house now being manufactured by many firms, including one in Germany, but the reader should make his own bird-houses. I am glad the

329

328

CROSS SECTION OF
STONE PIER

GATE POST

LOG

327

INVENTED &
DESIGNED BY
DAN BEARD

Gateways for game preserves, camps, etc.

Log gate and details of same.

manufacturers have taken up these ideas for the good they will *do the birds*, but the ideas were published first solely for the use of the boys in the hopes of educating them both in the conservation of bird life and in the manual training necessary to construct bird-houses.

The reader must have, no doubt, noticed that the problems in this book have become more and more difficult as we approach the end, but this is because everything grows; as we acquire skill we naturally seek more and more difficult work on which to exercise our skill. These gateways, however, are none of them too difficult for the boys to build themselves. The main problem to overcome in building the picturesque log gateway shown by Fig. 331 is not in laying up the logs or constructing the roof—the reader has already learned how to do both in the forepart of this book—but it is in so laying the logs that the slant or incline on the two outsides will be exactly the same, also in so building the sides that when you reach the top of the open way and place your first overhead log, the log will be exactly horizontal, exactly level, as it must be to carry out the plan in a workmanlike manner. Fig. 330 shows you the framework of the roof, the ridge-pole of which is a plank cut "sway-backed," that is, lower in the centre than at either end. The frame should be roofed with hand-rived shingles, or at least hand-trimmed shingles, if you use the manufactured article of commerce. This gateway is appropriate for a common post-and-rail fence or any of the log fences illustrated in the previous diagrams. Fig. 332 shows how the fence here shown is constructed: the *A* logs are bevelled to fit in diagonally, the *B* and *C* logs are set in as shown by the dotted line in Fig. 332. A gateway like the one shown here would make a splendid and imposing one for a permanent camp, whether it be a Boy Scout, a Girl Pioneer, a private camp for boys, or simply the entrance to a large private estate.

The writer has made these diagrams so that they may be used by men or boys; the last one shows a gateway large enough to admit a "four-in-hand" stage-coach or an automobile, but the boys may build it in miniature so that the opening is only large enough to admit a pedestrian.

The End

A CATALOG OF SELECTED DOVER BOOKS IN ALL FIELDS OF INTEREST

100 BEST-LOVED POEMS, Edited by Philip Smith. "The Passionate Shepherd to His Love," "Shall I compare thee to a summer's day?" "Death, be not proud," "The Raven," "The Road Not Taken," plus works by Blake, Wordsworth, Byron, Shelley, Keats, many others. 96pp. 5³⁄₁₆ x 8¼. 0-486-28553-7

100 SMALL HOUSES OF THE THIRTIES, Brown-Blodgett Company. Exterior photographs and floor plans for 100 charming structures. Illustrations of models accompanied by descriptions of interiors, color schemes, closet space, and other amenities. 200 illustrations. 112pp. 8⅜ x 11. 0-486-44131-8

1000 TURN-OF-THE-CENTURY HOUSES: With Illustrations and Floor Plans, Herbert C. Chivers. Reproduced from a rare edition, this showcase of homes ranges from cottages and bungalows to sprawling mansions. Each house is meticulously illustrated and accompanied by complete floor plans. 256pp. 9⅜ x 12¼.
0-486-45596-3

101 GREAT AMERICAN POEMS, Edited by The American Poetry & Literacy Project. Rich treasury of verse from the 19th and 20th centuries includes works by Edgar Allan Poe, Robert Frost, Walt Whitman, Langston Hughes, Emily Dickinson, T. S. Eliot, other notables. 96pp. 5³⁄₁₆ x 8¼. 0-486-40158-8

101 GREAT SAMURAI PRINTS, Utagawa Kuniyoshi. Kuniyoshi was a master of the warrior woodblock print — and these 18th-century illustrations represent the pinnacle of his craft. Full-color portraits of renowned Japanese samurais pulse with movement, passion, and remarkably fine detail. 112pp. 8⅜ x 11. 0-486-46523-3

ABC OF BALLET, Janet Grosser. Clearly worded, abundantly illustrated little guide defines basic ballet-related terms: arabesque, battement, pas de chat, relevé, sissonne, many others. Pronunciation guide included. Excellent primer. 48pp. 4³⁄₁₆ x 5¾.
0-486-40871-X

ACCESSORIES OF DRESS: An Illustrated Encyclopedia, Katherine Lester and Bess Viola Oerke. Illustrations of hats, veils, wigs, cravats, shawls, shoes, gloves, and other accessories enhance an engaging commentary that reveals the humor and charm of the many-sided story of accessorized apparel. 644 figures and 59 plates. 608pp. 6 ⅛ x 9¼.
0-486-43378-1

ADVENTURES OF HUCKLEBERRY FINN, Mark Twain. Join Huck and Jim as their boyhood adventures along the Mississippi River lead them into a world of excitement, danger, and self-discovery. Humorous narrative, lyrical descriptions of the Mississippi valley, and memorable characters. 224pp. 5³⁄₁₆ x 8¼. 0-486-28061-6

ALICE STARMORE'S BOOK OF FAIR ISLE KNITTING, Alice Starmore. A noted designer from the region of Scotland's Fair Isle explores the history and techniques of this distinctive, stranded-color knitting style and provides copious illustrated instructions for 14 original knitwear designs. 208pp. 8⅜ x 10⅞. 0-486-47218-3

Browse over 9,000 books at www.doverpublications.com

ALICE'S ADVENTURES IN WONDERLAND, Lewis Carroll. Beloved classic about a little girl lost in a topsy-turvy land and her encounters with the White Rabbit, March Hare, Mad Hatter, Cheshire Cat, and other delightfully improbable characters. 42 illustrations by Sir John Tenniel. 96pp. 5³⁄₁₆ x 8¼. 0-486-27543-4

AMERICA'S LIGHTHOUSES: An Illustrated History, Francis Ross Holland. Profusely illustrated fact-filled survey of American lighthouses since 1716. Over 200 stations — East, Gulf, and West coasts, Great Lakes, Hawaii, Alaska, Puerto Rico, the Virgin Islands, and the Mississippi and St. Lawrence Rivers. 240pp. 8 x 10¾. 0-486-25576-X

AN ENCYCLOPEDIA OF THE VIOLIN, Alberto Bachmann. Translated by Frederick H. Martens. Introduction by Eugene Ysaye. First published in 1925, this renowned reference remains unsurpassed as a source of essential information, from construction and evolution to repertoire and technique. Includes a glossary and 73 illustrations. 496pp. 6⅛ x 9¼. 0-486-46618-3

ANIMALS: 1,419 Copyright-Free Illustrations of Mammals, Birds, Fish, Insects, etc., Selected by Jim Harter. Selected for its visual impact and ease of use, this outstanding collection of wood engravings presents over 1,000 species of animals in extremely lifelike poses. Includes mammals, birds, reptiles, amphibians, fish, insects, and other invertebrates. 284pp. 9 x 12. 0-486-23766-4

THE ANNALS, Tacitus. Translated by Alfred John Church and William Jackson Brodribb. This vital chronicle of Imperial Rome, written by the era's great historian, spans A.D. 14-68 and paints incisive psychological portraits of major figures, from Tiberius to Nero. 416pp. 5³⁄₁₆ x 8¼. 0-486-45236-0

ANTIGONE, Sophocles. Filled with passionate speeches and sensitive probing of moral and philosophical issues, this powerful and often-performed Greek drama reveals the grim fate that befalls the children of Oedipus. Footnotes. 64pp. 5³⁄₁₆ x 8 ¼. 0-486-27804-2

ART DECO DECORATIVE PATTERNS IN FULL COLOR, Christian Stoll. Reprinted from a rare 1910 portfolio, 160 sensuous and exotic images depict a breathtaking array of florals, geometrics, and abstracts — all elegant in their stark simplicity. 64pp. 8⅜ x 11. 0-486-44862-2

THE ARTHUR RACKHAM TREASURY: 86 Full-Color Illustrations, Arthur Rackham. Selected and Edited by Jeff A. Menges. A stunning treasury of 86 full-page plates span the famed English artist's career, from *Rip Van Winkle* (1905) to masterworks such as *Undine, A Midsummer Night's Dream,* and *Wind in the Willows* (1939). 96pp. 8⅜ x 11. 0-486-44685-9

THE AUTHENTIC GILBERT & SULLIVAN SONGBOOK, W. S. Gilbert and A. S. Sullivan. The most comprehensive collection available, this songbook includes selections from every one of Gilbert and Sullivan's light operas. Ninety-two numbers are presented uncut and unedited, and in their original keys. 410pp. 9 x 12. 0-486-23482-7

THE AWAKENING, Kate Chopin. First published in 1899, this controversial novel of a New Orleans wife's search for love outside a stifling marriage shocked readers. Today, it remains a first-rate narrative with superb characterization. New introductory Note. 128pp. 5³⁄₁₆ x 8¼. 0-486-27786-0

BASIC DRAWING, Louis Priscilla. Beginning with perspective, this commonsense manual progresses to the figure in movement, light and shade, anatomy, drapery, composition, trees and landscape, and outdoor sketching. Black-and-white illustrations throughout. 128pp. 8⅜ x 11. 0-486-45815-6

Browse over 9,000 books at www.doverpublications.com

THE BATTLES THAT CHANGED HISTORY, Fletcher Pratt. Historian profiles 16 crucial conflicts, ancient to modern, that changed the course of Western civilization. Gripping accounts of battles led by Alexander the Great, Joan of Arc, Ulysses S. Grant, other commanders. 27 maps. 352pp. 5⅜ x 8½.   0-486-41129-X

BEETHOVEN'S LETTERS, Ludwig van Beethoven. Edited by Dr. A. C. Kalischer. Features 457 letters to fellow musicians, friends, greats, patrons, and literary men. Reveals musical thoughts, quirks of personality, insights, and daily events. Includes 15 plates. 410pp. 5⅜ x 8½.   0-486-22769-3

BERNICE BOBS HER HAIR AND OTHER STORIES, F. Scott Fitzgerald. This brilliant anthology includes 6 of Fitzgerald's most popular stories: "The Diamond as Big as the Ritz," the title tale, "The Offshore Pirate," "The Ice Palace," "The Jelly Bean," and "May Day." 176pp. 5⅜ x 8½.   0-486-47049-0

BESLER'S BOOK OF FLOWERS AND PLANTS: 73 Full-Color Plates from Hortus Eystettensis, 1613, Basilius Besler. Here is a selection of magnificent plates from the Hortus Eystettensis, which vividly illustrated and identified the plants, flowers, and trees that thrived in the legendary German garden at Eichstätt. 80pp. 8⅜ x 11.
0-486-46005-3

THE BOOK OF KELLS, Edited by Blanche Cirker. Painstakingly reproduced from a rare facsimile edition, this volume contains full-page decorations, portraits, illustrations, plus a sampling of textual leaves with exquisite calligraphy and ornamentation. 32 full-color illustrations. 32pp. 9⅜ x 12¼.   0-486-24345-1

THE BOOK OF THE CROSSBOW: With an Additional Section on Catapults and Other Siege Engines, Ralph Payne-Gallwey. Fascinating study traces history and use of crossbow as military and sporting weapon, from Middle Ages to modern times. Also covers related weapons: balistas, catapults, Turkish bows, more. Over 240 illustrations. 400pp. 7¼ x 10⅛.   0-486-28720-3

THE BUNGALOW BOOK: Floor Plans and Photos of 112 Houses, 1910, Henry L. Wilson. Here are 112 of the most popular and economic blueprints of the early 20th century — plus an illustration or photograph of each completed house. A wonderful time capsule that still offers a wealth of valuable insights. 160pp. 8⅜ x 11.
0-486-45104-6

THE CALL OF THE WILD, Jack London. A classic novel of adventure, drawn from London's own experiences as a Klondike adventurer, relating the story of a heroic dog caught in the brutal life of the Alaska Gold Rush. Note. 64pp. 5³⁄₁₆ x 8¼.
0-486-26472-6

CANDIDE, Voltaire. Edited by Francois-Marie Arouet. One of the world's great satires since its first publication in 1759. Witty, caustic skewering of romance, science, philosophy, religion, government — nearly all human ideals and institutions. 112pp. 5³⁄₁₆ x 8¼.   0-486-26689-3

CELEBRATED IN THEIR TIME: Photographic Portraits from the George Grantham Bain Collection, Edited by Amy Pastan. With an Introduction by Michael Carlebach. Remarkable portrait gallery features 112 rare images of Albert Einstein, Charlie Chaplin, the Wright Brothers, Henry Ford, and other luminaries from the worlds of politics, art, entertainment, and industry. 128pp. 8⅜ x 11.   0-486-46754-6

CHARIOTS FOR APOLLO: The NASA History of Manned Lunar Spacecraft to 1969, Courtney G. Brooks, James M. Grimwood, and Loyd S. Swenson, Jr. This illustrated history by a trio of experts is the definitive reference on the Apollo spacecraft and lunar modules. It traces the vehicles' design, development, and operation in space. More than 100 photographs and illustrations. 576pp. 6¾ x 9¼. 0-486-46756-2

Browse over 9,000 books at www.doverpublications.com

A CHRISTMAS CAROL, Charles Dickens. This engrossing tale relates Ebenezer Scrooge's ghostly journeys through Christmases past, present, and future and his ultimate transformation from a harsh and grasping old miser to a charitable and compassionate human being. 80pp. 5¾₆ x 8¼.

0-486-26865-9

COMMON SENSE, Thomas Paine. First published in January of 1776, this highly influential landmark document clearly and persuasively argued for American separation from Great Britain and paved the way for the Declaration of Independence. 64pp. 5¾₆ x 8¼.

0-486-29602-4

THE COMPLETE SHORT STORIES OF OSCAR WILDE, Oscar Wilde. Complete texts of "The Happy Prince and Other Tales," "A House of Pomegranates," "Lord Arthur Savile's Crime and Other Stories," "Poems in Prose," and "The Portrait of Mr. W. H." 208pp. 5¾₆ x 8¼.

0-486-45216-6

COMPLETE SONNETS, William Shakespeare. Over 150 exquisite poems deal with love, friendship, the tyranny of time, beauty's evanescence, death, and other themes in language of remarkable power, precision, and beauty. Glossary of archaic terms. 80pp. 5¾₆ x 8¼.

0-486-26686-9

THE COUNT OF MONTE CRISTO: Abridged Edition, Alexandre Dumas. Falsely accused of treason, Edmond Dantès is imprisoned in the bleak Chateau d'If. After a hair-raising escape, he launches an elaborate plot to extract a bitter revenge against those who betrayed him. 448pp. 5¾₆ x 8¼.

0-486-45643-9

CRAFTSMAN BUNGALOWS: Designs from the Pacific Northwest, Yoho & Merritt. This reprint of a rare catalog, showcasing the charming simplicity and cozy style of Craftsman bungalows, is filled with photos of completed homes, plus floor plans and estimated costs. An indispensable resource for architects, historians, and illustrators. 112pp. 10 x 7.

0-486-46875-5

CRAFTSMAN BUNGALOWS: 59 Homes from "The Craftsman," Edited by Gustav Stickley. Best and most attractive designs from Arts and Crafts Movement publication — 1903–1916 — includes sketches, photographs of homes, floor plans, descriptive text. 128pp. 8¼ x 11.

0-486-25829-7

CRIME AND PUNISHMENT, Fyodor Dostoyevsky. Translated by Constance Garnett. Supreme masterpiece tells the story of Raskolnikov, a student tormented by his own thoughts after he murders an old woman. Overwhelmed by guilt and terror, he confesses and goes to prison. 480pp. 5¾₆ x 8¼.

0-486-41587-2

THE DECLARATION OF INDEPENDENCE AND OTHER GREAT DOCUMENTS OF AMERICAN HISTORY: 1775-1865, Edited by John Grafton. Thirteen compelling and influential documents: Henry's "Give Me Liberty or Give Me Death," Declaration of Independence, The Constitution, Washington's First Inaugural Address, The Monroe Doctrine, The Emancipation Proclamation, Gettysburg Address, more. 64pp. 5¾₆ x 8¼.

0-486-41124-9

THE DESERT AND THE SOWN: Travels in Palestine and Syria, Gertrude Bell. "The female Lawrence of Arabia," Gertrude Bell wrote captivating, perceptive accounts of her travels in the Middle East. This intriguing narrative, accompanied by 160 photos, traces her 1905 sojourn in Lebanon, Syria, and Palestine. 368pp. 5⅜ x 8½.

0-486-46876-3

A DOLL'S HOUSE, Henrik Ibsen. Ibsen's best-known play displays his genius for realistic prose drama. An expression of women's rights, the play climaxes when the central character, Nora, rejects a smothering marriage and life in "a doll's house." 80pp. 5¾₆ x 8¼.

0-486-27062-9

Browse over 9,000 books at www.doverpublications.com

DOOMED SHIPS: Great Ocean Liner Disasters, William H. Miller, Jr. Nearly 200 photographs, many from private collections, highlight tales of some of the vessels whose pleasure cruises ended in catastrophe: the *Morro Castle, Normandie, Andrea Doria, Europa,* and many others. 128pp. 8⅞ x 11¾. 0-486-45366-9

THE DORÉ BIBLE ILLUSTRATIONS, Gustave Doré. Detailed plates from the Bible: the Creation scenes, Adam and Eve, horrifying visions of the Flood, the battle sequences with their monumental crowds, depictions of the life of Jesus, 241 plates in all. 241pp. 9 x 12. 0-486-23004-X

DRAWING DRAPERY FROM HEAD TO TOE, Cliff Young. Expert guidance on how to draw shirts, pants, skirts, gloves, hats, and coats on the human figure, including folds in relation to the body, pull and crush, action folds, creases, more. Over 200 drawings. 48pp. 8¼ x 11. 0-486-45591-2

DUBLINERS, James Joyce. A fine and accessible introduction to the work of one of the 20th century's most influential writers, this collection features 15 tales, including a masterpiece of the short-story genre, "The Dead." 160pp. 5³⁄₁₆ x 8¼. 0-486-26870-5

EASY-TO-MAKE POP-UPS, Joan Irvine. Illustrated by Barbara Reid. Dozens of wonderful ideas for three-dimensional paper fun — from holiday greeting cards with moving parts to a pop-up menagerie. Easy-to-follow, illustrated instructions for more than 30 projects. 299 black-and-white illustrations. 96pp. 8⅜ x 11. 0-486-44622-0

EASY-TO-MAKE STORYBOOK DOLLS: A "Novel" Approach to Cloth Dollmaking, Sherralyn St. Clair. Favorite fictional characters come alive in this unique beginner's dollmaking guide. Includes patterns for Pollyanna, Dorothy from *The Wonderful Wizard of Oz,* Mary of *The Secret Garden,* plus easy-to-follow instructions, 263 black-and-white illustrations, and an 8-page color insert. 112pp. 8¼ x 11. 0-486-47360-0

EINSTEIN'S ESSAYS IN SCIENCE, Albert Einstein. Speeches and essays in accessible, everyday language profile influential physicists such as Niels Bohr and Isaac Newton. They also explore areas of physics to which the author made major contributions. 128pp. 5 x 8. 0-486-47011-3

EL DORADO: Further Adventures of the Scarlet Pimpernel, Baroness Orczy. A popular sequel to *The Scarlet Pimpernel,* this suspenseful story recounts the Pimpernel's attempts to rescue the Dauphin from imprisonment during the French Revolution. An irresistible blend of intrigue, period detail, and vibrant characterizations. 352pp. 5³⁄₁₆ x 8¼. 0-486-44026-5

ELEGANT SMALL HOMES OF THE TWENTIES: 99 Designs from a Competition, Chicago Tribune. Nearly 100 designs for five- and six-room houses feature New England and Southern colonials, Normandy cottages, stately Italianate dwellings, and other fascinating snapshots of American domestic architecture of the 1920s. 112pp. 9 x 12. 0-486-46910-7

THE ELEMENTS OF STYLE: The Original Edition, William Strunk, Jr. This is the book that generations of writers have relied upon for timeless advice on grammar, diction, syntax, and other essentials. In concise terms, it identifies the principal requirements of proper style and common errors. 64pp. 5⅜ x 8½. 0-486-44798-7

THE ELUSIVE PIMPERNEL, Baroness Orczy. Robespierre's revolutionaries find their wicked schemes thwarted by the heroic Pimpernel — Sir Percival Blakeney. In this thrilling sequel, Chauvelin devises a plot to eliminate the Pimpernel and his wife. 272pp. 5³⁄₁₆ x 8¼. 0-486-45464-9

AN ENCYCLOPEDIA OF BATTLES: Accounts of Over 1,560 Battles from 1479 B.C. to the Present, David Eggenberger. Essential details of every major battle in recorded history from the first battle of Megiddo in 1479 B.C. to Grenada in 1984. List of battle maps. 99 illustrations. 544pp. 6½ x 9¼. 0-486-24913-1

ENCYCLOPEDIA OF EMBROIDERY STITCHES, INCLUDING CREWEL, Marion Nichols. Precise explanations and instructions, clearly illustrated, on how to work chain, back, cross, knotted, woven stitches, and many more — 178 in all, including Cable Outline, Whipped Satin, and Eyelet Buttonhole. Over 1400 illustrations. 219pp. 8⅜ x 11¼. 0-486-22929-7

ENTER JEEVES: 15 Early Stories, P. G. Wodehouse. Splendid collection contains first 8 stories featuring Bertie Wooster, the deliciously dim aristocrat and Jeeves, his brainy, imperturbable manservant. Also, the complete Reggie Pepper (Bertie's prototype) series. 288pp. 5⅜ x 8½. 0-486-29717-9

ERIC SLOANE'S AMERICA: Paintings in Oil, Michael Wigley. With a Foreword by Mimi Sloane. Eric Sloane's evocative oils of America's landscape and material culture shimmer with immense historical and nostalgic appeal. This original hardcover collection gathers nearly a hundred of his finest paintings, with subjects ranging from New England to the American Southwest. 128pp. 10⅜ x 9. 0-486-46525-X

ETHAN FROME, Edith Wharton. Classic story of wasted lives, set against a bleak New England background. Superbly delineated characters in a hauntingly grim tale of thwarted love. Considered by many to be Wharton's masterpiece. 96pp. 5³⁄₁₆ x 8 ¼. 0-486-26690-7

THE EVERLASTING MAN, G. K. Chesterton. Chesterton's view of Christianity — as a blend of philosophy and mythology, satisfying intellect and spirit — applies to his brilliant book, which appeals to readers' heads as well as their hearts. 288pp. 5⅜ x 8½. 0-486-46036-3

THE FIELD AND FOREST HANDY BOOK, Daniel Beard. Written by a co-founder of the Boy Scouts, this appealing guide offers illustrated instructions for building kites, birdhouses, boats, igloos, and other fun projects, plus numerous helpful tips for campers. 448pp. 5³⁄₁₆ x 8¼. 0-486-46191-2

FINDING YOUR WAY WITHOUT MAP OR COMPASS, Harold Gatty. Useful, instructive manual shows would-be explorers, hikers, bikers, scouts, sailors, and survivalists how to find their way outdoors by observing animals, weather patterns, shifting sands, and other elements of nature. 288pp. 5⅜ x 8½. 0-486-40613-X

FIRST FRENCH READER: A Beginner's Dual-Language Book, Edited and Translated by Stanley Appelbaum. This anthology introduces 50 legendary writers — Voltaire, Balzac, Baudelaire, Proust, more — through passages from *The Red and the Black, Les Misérables, Madame Bovary,* and other classics. Original French text plus English translation on facing pages. 240pp. 5⅜ x 8½. 0-486-46178-5

FIRST GERMAN READER: A Beginner's Dual-Language Book, Edited by Harry Steinhauer. Specially chosen for their power to evoke German life and culture, these short, simple readings include poems, stories, essays, and anecdotes by Goethe, Hesse, Heine, Schiller, and others. 224pp. 5⅜ x 8½. 0-486-46179-3

FIRST SPANISH READER: A Beginner's Dual-Language Book, Angel Flores. Delightful stories, other material based on works of Don Juan Manuel, Luis Taboada, Ricardo Palma, other noted writers. Complete faithful English translations on facing pages. Exercises. 176pp. 5⅜ x 8½. 0-486-25810-6

Browse over 9,000 books at www.doverpublications.com

FIVE ACRES AND INDEPENDENCE, Maurice G. Kains. Great back-to-the-land classic explains basics of self-sufficient farming. The one book to get. 95 illustrations. 397pp. 5⅜ x 8½.   0-486-20974-1

FLAGG'S SMALL HOUSES: Their Economic Design and Construction, 1922, Ernest Flagg. Although most famous for his skyscrapers, Flagg was also a proponent of the well-designed single-family dwelling. His classic treatise features innovations that save space, materials, and cost. 526 illustrations. 160pp. 9⅜ x 12¼.
0-486-45197-6

FLATLAND: A Romance of Many Dimensions, Edwin A. Abbott. Classic of science (and mathematical) fiction — charmingly illustrated by the author — describes the adventures of A. Square, a resident of Flatland, in Spaceland (three dimensions), Lineland (one dimension), and Pointland (no dimensions). 96pp. 5³⁄₁₆ x 8¼.
0-486-27263-X

FRANKENSTEIN, Mary Shelley. The story of Victor Frankenstein's monstrous creation and the havoc it caused has enthralled generations of readers and inspired countless writers of horror and suspense. With the author's own 1831 introduction. 176pp. 5³⁄₁₆ x 8¼.   0-486-28211-2

THE GARGOYLE BOOK: 572 Examples from Gothic Architecture, Lester Burbank Bridaham. Dispelling the conventional wisdom that French Gothic architectural flourishes were born of despair or gloom, Bridaham reveals the whimsical nature of these creations and the ingenious artisans who made them. 572 illustrations. 224pp. 8⅜ x 11.   0-486-44754-5

THE GIFT OF THE MAGI AND OTHER SHORT STORIES, O. Henry. Sixteen captivating stories by one of America's most popular storytellers. Included are such classics as "The Gift of the Magi," "The Last Leaf," and "The Ransom of Red Chief." Publisher's Note. 96pp. 5³⁄₁₆ x 8¼.   0-486-27061-0

THE GOETHE TREASURY: Selected Prose and Poetry, Johann Wolfgang von Goethe. Edited, Selected, and with an Introduction by Thomas Mann. In addition to his lyric poetry, Goethe wrote travel sketches, autobiographical studies, essays, letters, and proverbs in rhyme and prose. This collection presents outstanding examples from each genre. 368pp. 5⅜ x 8½.   0-486-44780-4

GREAT EXPECTATIONS, Charles Dickens. Orphaned Pip is apprenticed to the dirty work of the forge but dreams of becoming a gentleman — and one day finds himself in possession of "great expectations." Dickens' finest novel. 400pp. 5³⁄₁₆ x 8¼.
0-486-41586-4

GREAT WRITERS ON THE ART OF FICTION: From Mark Twain to Joyce Carol Oates, Edited by James Daley. An indispensable source of advice and inspiration, this anthology features essays by Henry James, Kate Chopin, Willa Cather, Sinclair Lewis, Jack London, Raymond Chandler, Raymond Carver, Eudora Welty, and Kurt Vonnegut, Jr. 192pp. 5⅜ x 8½.   0-486-45128-3

HAMLET, William Shakespeare. The quintessential Shakespearean tragedy, whose highly charged confrontations and anguished soliloquies probe depths of human feeling rarely sounded in any art. Reprinted from an authoritative British edition complete with illuminating footnotes. 128pp. 5³⁄₁₆ x 8¼.   0-486-27278-8

THE HAUNTED HOUSE, Charles Dickens. A Yuletide gathering in an eerie country retreat provides the backdrop for Dickens and his friends — including Elizabeth Gaskell and Wilkie Collins — who take turns spinning supernatural yarns. 144pp. 5⅜ x 8½.   0-486-46309-5

HEART OF DARKNESS, Joseph Conrad. Dark allegory of a journey up the Congo River and the narrator's encounter with the mysterious Mr. Kurtz. Masterly blend of adventure, character study, psychological penetration. For many, Conrad's finest, most enigmatic story. 80pp. 5³⁄₁₆ x 8¼. 0-486-26464-5

HENSON AT THE NORTH POLE, Matthew A. Henson. This thrilling memoir by the heroic African-American who was Peary's companion through two decades of Arctic exploration recounts a tale of danger, courage, and determination. "Fascinating and exciting." — *Commonweal.* 128pp. 5⅜ x 8½. 0-486-45472-X

HISTORIC COSTUMES AND HOW TO MAKE THEM, Mary Fernald and E. Shenton. Practical, informative guidebook shows how to create everything from short tunics worn by Saxon men in the fifth century to a lady's bustle dress of the late 1800s. 81 illustrations. 176pp. 5⅜ x 8½. 0-486-44906-8

THE HOUND OF THE BASKERVILLES, Arthur Conan Doyle. A deadly curse in the form of a legendary ferocious beast continues to claim its victims from the Baskerville family until Holmes and Watson intervene. Often called the best detective story ever written. 128pp. 5³⁄₁₆ x 8¼. 0-486-28214-7

THE HOUSE BEHIND THE CEDARS, Charles W. Chesnutt. Originally published in 1900, this groundbreaking novel by a distinguished African-American author recounts the drama of a brother and sister who "pass for white" during the dangerous days of Reconstruction. 208pp. 5⅜ x 8½. 0-486-46144-0

THE HUMAN FIGURE IN MOTION, Eadweard Muybridge. The 4,789 photographs in this definitive selection show the human figure — models almost all undraped — engaged in over 160 different types of action: running, climbing stairs, etc. 390pp. 7⅞ x 10⅝. 0-486-20204-6

THE IMPORTANCE OF BEING EARNEST, Oscar Wilde. Wilde's witty and buoyant comedy of manners, filled with some of literature's most famous epigrams, reprinted from an authoritative British edition. Considered Wilde's most perfect work. 64pp. 5³⁄₁₆ x 8¼. 0-486-26478-5

THE INFERNO, Dante Alighieri. Translated and with notes by Henry Wadsworth Longfellow. The first stop on Dante's famous journey from Hell to Purgatory to Paradise, this 14th-century allegorical poem blends vivid and shocking imagery with graceful lyricism. Translated by the beloved 19th-century poet, Henry Wadsworth Longfellow. 256pp. 5³⁄₁₆ x 8¼. 0-486-44288-8

JANE EYRE, Charlotte Brontë. Written in 1847, *Jane Eyre* tells the tale of an orphan girl's progress from the custody of cruel relatives to an oppressive boarding school and its culmination in a troubled career as a governess. 448pp. 5³⁄₁₆ x 8¼.
0-486-42449-9

JAPANESE WOODBLOCK FLOWER PRINTS, Tanigami Kônan. Extraordinary collection of Japanese woodblock prints by a well-known artist features 120 plates in brilliant color. Realistic images from a rare edition include daffodils, tulips, and other familiar and unusual flowers. 128pp. 11 x 8¼. 0-486-46442-3

JEWELRY MAKING AND DESIGN, Augustus F. Rose and Antonio Cirino. Professional secrets of jewelry making are revealed in a thorough, practical guide. Over 200 illustrations. 306pp. 5⅜ x 8½. 0-486-21750-7

JULIUS CAESAR, William Shakespeare. Great tragedy based on Plutarch's account of the lives of Brutus, Julius Caesar and Mark Antony. Evil plotting, ringing oratory, high tragedy with Shakespeare's incomparable insight, dramatic power. Explanatory footnotes. 96pp. 5³⁄₁₆ x 8¼. 0-486-26876-4

Browse over 9,000 books at www.doverpublications.com

THE JUNGLE, Upton Sinclair. 1906 bestseller shockingly reveals intolerable labor practices and working conditions in the Chicago stockyards as it tells the grim story of a Slavic family that emigrates to America full of optimism but soon faces despair. 320pp. 5³/₁₆ x 8¼. 0-486-41923-1

THE KINGDOM OF GOD IS WITHIN YOU, Leo Tolstoy. The soul-searching book that inspired Gandhi to embrace the concept of passive resistance, Tolstoy's 1894 polemic clearly outlines a radical, well-reasoned revision of traditional Christian thinking. 352pp. 5³/₁₆ x 8¼. 0-486-45138-0

THE LADY OR THE TIGER?: and Other Logic Puzzles, Raymond M. Smullyan. Created by a renowned puzzle master, these whimsically themed challenges involve paradoxes about probability, time, and change; metapuzzles; and self-referentiality. Nineteen chapters advance in difficulty from relatively simple to highly complex. 1982 edition. 240pp. 5⅜ x 8½. 0-486-47027-X

LEAVES OF GRASS: The Original 1855 Edition, Walt Whitman. Whitman's immortal collection includes some of the greatest poems of modern times, including his masterpiece, "Song of Myself." Shattering standard conventions, it stands as an unabashed celebration of body and nature. 128pp. 5³/₁₆ x 8¼. 0-486-45676-5

LES MISÉRABLES, Victor Hugo. Translated by Charles E. Wilbour. Abridged by James K. Robinson. A convict's heroic struggle for justice and redemption plays out against a fiery backdrop of the Napoleonic wars. This edition features the excellent original translation and a sensitive abridgment. 304pp. 6⅛ x 9¼.
0-486-45789-3

LILITH: A Romance, George MacDonald. In this novel by the father of fantasy literature, a man travels through time to meet Adam and Eve and to explore humanity's fall from grace and ultimate redemption. 240pp. 5⅜ x 8½.
0-486-46818-6

THE LOST LANGUAGE OF SYMBOLISM, Harold Bayley. This remarkable book reveals the hidden meaning behind familiar images and words, from the origins of Santa Claus to the fleur-de-lys, drawing from mythology, folklore, religious texts, and fairy tales. 1,418 illustrations. 784pp. 5⅜ x 8½. 0-486-44787-1

MACBETH, William Shakespeare. A Scottish nobleman murders the king in order to succeed to the throne. Tortured by his conscience and fearful of discovery, he becomes tangled in a web of treachery and deceit that ultimately spells his doom. 96pp. 5³/₁₆ x 8¼. 0-486-27802-6

MAKING AUTHENTIC CRAFTSMAN FURNITURE: Instructions and Plans for 62 Projects, Gustav Stickley. Make authentic reproductions of handsome, functional, durable furniture: tables, chairs, wall cabinets, desks, a hall tree, and more. Construction plans with drawings, schematics, dimensions, and lumber specs reprinted from 1900s The Craftsman magazine. 128pp. 8⅛ x 11. 0-486-25000-8

MATHEMATICS FOR THE NONMATHEMATICIAN, Morris Kline. Erudite and entertaining overview follows development of mathematics from ancient Greeks to present. Topics include logic and mathematics, the fundamental concept, differential calculus, probability theory, much more. Exercises and problems. 641pp. 5⅜ x 8½. 0-486-24823-2

MEMOIRS OF AN ARABIAN PRINCESS FROM ZANZIBAR, Emily Ruete. This 19th-century autobiography offers a rare inside look at the society surrounding a sultan's palace. A real-life princess in exile recalls her vanished world of harems, slave trading, and court intrigues. 288pp. 5⅜ x 8½. 0-486-47121-7

Browse over 9,000 books at www.doverpublications.com

THE METAMORPHOSIS AND OTHER STORIES, Franz Kafka. Excellent new English translations of title story (considered by many critics Kafka's most perfect work), plus "The Judgment," "In the Penal Colony," "A Country Doctor," and "A Report to an Academy." Note. 96pp. 5⅜₆ x 8¼.   0-486-29030-1

MICROSCOPIC ART FORMS FROM THE PLANT WORLD, R. Anheisser. From undulating curves to complex geometrics, a world of fascinating images abound in this classic, illustrated survey of microscopic plants. Features 400 detailed illustrations of nature's minute but magnificent handiwork. The accompanying CD-ROM includes all of the images in the book. 128pp. 9 x 9.   0-486-46013-4

A MIDSUMMER NIGHT'S DREAM, William Shakespeare. Among the most popular of Shakespeare's comedies, this enchanting play humorously celebrates the vagaries of love as it focuses upon the intertwined romances of several pairs of lovers. Explanatory footnotes. 80pp. 5⅜₆ x 8¼.   0-486-27067-X

THE MONEY CHANGERS, Upton Sinclair. Originally published in 1908, this cautionary novel from the author of *The Jungle* explores corruption within the American system as a group of power brokers joins forces for personal gain, triggering a crash on Wall Street. 192pp. 5⅜ x 8½.   0-486-46917-4

THE MOST POPULAR HOMES OF THE TWENTIES, William A. Radford. With a New Introduction by Daniel D. Reiff. Based on a rare 1925 catalog, this architectural showcase features floor plans, construction details, and photos of 26 homes, plus articles on entrances, porches, garages, and more. 250 illustrations, 21 color plates. 176pp. 8⅜ x 11.   0-486-47028-8

MY 66 YEARS IN THE BIG LEAGUES, Connie Mack. With a New Introduction by Rich Westcott. A Founding Father of modern baseball, Mack holds the record for most wins — and losses — by a major league manager. Enhanced by 70 photographs, his warmhearted autobiography is populated by many legends of the game. 288pp. 5⅜ x 8½.   0-486-47184-5

NARRATIVE OF THE LIFE OF FREDERICK DOUGLASS, Frederick Douglass. Douglass's graphic depictions of slavery, harrowing escape to freedom, and life as a newspaper editor, eloquent orator, and impassioned abolitionist. 96pp. 5⅜₆ x 8¼.
0-486-28499-9

THE NIGHTLESS CITY: Geisha and Courtesan Life in Old Tokyo, J. E. de Becker. This unsurpassed study from 100 years ago ventured into Tokyo's red-light district to survey geisha and courtesan life and offer meticulous descriptions of training, dress, social hierarchy, and erotic practices. 49 black-and-white illustrations; 2 maps. 496pp. 5⅜ x 8½.   0-486-45563-7

THE ODYSSEY, Homer. Excellent prose translation of ancient epic recounts adventures of the homeward-bound Odysseus. Fantastic cast of gods, giants, cannibals, sirens, other supernatural creatures — true classic of Western literature. 256pp. 5⅜₆ x 8¼.
0-486-40654-7

OEDIPUS REX, Sophocles. Landmark of Western drama concerns the catastrophe that ensues when King Oedipus discovers he has inadvertently killed his father and married his mother. Masterly construction, dramatic irony. Explanatory footnotes. 64pp. 5⅜₆ x 8¼.   0-486-26877-2

ONCE UPON A TIME: The Way America Was, Eric Sloane. Nostalgic text and drawings brim with gentle philosophies and descriptions of how we used to live — self-sufficiently — on the land, in homes, and among the things built by hand. 44 line illustrations. 64pp. 8⅜ x 11.   0-486-44411-2

ONE OF OURS, Willa Cather. The Pulitzer Prize–winning novel about a young Nebraskan looking for something to believe in. Alienated from his parents, rejected by his wife, he finds his destiny on the bloody battlefields of World War I. 352pp. 5³⁄₁₆ x 8¼. 0-486-45599-8

ORIGAMI YOU CAN USE: 27 Practical Projects, Rick Beech. Origami models can be more than decorative, and this unique volume shows how! The 27 practical projects include a CD case, frame, napkin ring, and dish. Easy instructions feature 400 two-color illustrations. 96pp. 8¼ x 11. 0-486-47057-1

OTHELLO, William Shakespeare. Towering tragedy tells the story of a Moorish general who earns the enmity of his ensign Iago when he passes him over for a promotion. Masterly portrait of an archvillain. Explanatory footnotes. 112pp. 5³⁄₁₆ x 8¼. 0-486-29097-2

PARADISE LOST, John Milton. Notes by John A. Himes. First published in 1667, *Paradise Lost* ranks among the greatest of English literature's epic poems. It's a sublime retelling of Adam and Eve's fall from grace and expulsion from Eden. Notes by John A. Himes. 480pp. 5³⁄₁₆ x 8¼. 0-486-44287-X

PASSING, Nella Larsen. Married to a successful physician and prominently ensconced in society, Irene Redfield leads a charmed existence — until a chance encounter with a childhood friend who has been "passing for white." 112pp. 5⅜ x 8½. 0-486-43713-2

PERSPECTIVE DRAWING FOR BEGINNERS, Len A. Doust. Doust carefully explains the roles of lines, boxes, and circles, and shows how visualizing shapes and forms can be used in accurate depictions of perspective. One of the most concise introductions available. 33 illustrations. 64pp. 5⅜ x 8½. 0-486-45149-6

PERSPECTIVE MADE EASY, Ernest R. Norling. Perspective is easy; yet, surprisingly few artists know the simple rules that make it so. Remedy that situation with this simple, step-by-step book, the first devoted entirely to the topic. 256 illustrations. 224pp. 5⅜ x 8½. 0-486-40473-0

THE PICTURE OF DORIAN GRAY, Oscar Wilde. Celebrated novel involves a handsome young Londoner who sinks into a life of depravity. His body retains perfect youth and vigor while his recent portrait reflects the ravages of his crime and sensuality. 176pp. 5³⁄₁₆ x 8¼. 0-486-27807-7

PRIDE AND PREJUDICE, Jane Austen. One of the most universally loved and admired English novels, an effervescent tale of rural romance transformed by Jane Austen's art into a witty, shrewdly observed satire of English country life. 272pp. 5³⁄₁₆ x 8¼. 0-486-28473-5

THE PRINCE, Niccolò Machiavelli. Classic, Renaissance-era guide to acquiring and maintaining political power. Today, nearly 500 years after it was written, this calculating prescription for autocratic rule continues to be much read and studied. 80pp. 5³⁄₁₆ x 8¼. 0-486-27274-5

QUICK SKETCHING, Carl Cheek. A perfect introduction to the technique of "quick sketching." Drawing upon an artist's immediate emotional responses, this is an extremely effective means of capturing the essential form and features of a subject. More than 100 black-and-white illustrations throughout. 48pp. 11 x 8¼. 0-486-46608-6

RANCH LIFE AND THE HUNTING TRAIL, Theodore Roosevelt. Illustrated by Frederic Remington. Beautifully illustrated by Remington, Roosevelt's celebration of the Old West recounts his adventures in the Dakota Badlands of the 1880s, from round-ups to Indian encounters to hunting bighorn sheep. 208pp. 6¼ x 9¼. 0-486-47340-6

THE RED BADGE OF COURAGE, Stephen Crane. Amid the nightmarish chaos of a Civil War battle, a young soldier discovers courage, humility, and, perhaps, wisdom. Uncanny re-creation of actual combat. Enduring landmark of American fiction. 112pp. 5³⁄₁₆ x 8¼. 0-486-26465-3

RELATIVITY SIMPLY EXPLAINED, Martin Gardner. One of the subject's clearest, most entertaining introductions offers lucid explanations of special and general theories of relativity, gravity, and spacetime, models of the universe, and more. 100 illustrations. 224pp. 5⅜ x 8½. 0-486-29315-7

REMBRANDT DRAWINGS: 116 Masterpieces in Original Color, Rembrandt van Rijn. This deluxe hardcover edition features drawings from throughout the Dutch master's prolific career. Informative captions accompany these beautifully reproduced landscapes, biblical vignettes, figure studies, animal sketches, and portraits. 128pp. 8⅜ x 11. 0-486-46149-1

THE ROAD NOT TAKEN AND OTHER POEMS, Robert Frost. A treasury of Frost's most expressive verse. In addition to the title poem: "An Old Man's Winter Night," "In the Home Stretch," "Meeting and Passing," "Putting in the Seed," many more. All complete and unabridged. 64pp. 5³⁄₁₆ x 8¼. 0-486-27550-7

ROMEO AND JULIET, William Shakespeare. Tragic tale of star-crossed lovers, feuding families and timeless passion contains some of Shakespeare's most beautiful and lyrical love poetry. Complete, unabridged text with explanatory footnotes. 96pp. 5³⁄₁₆ x 8¼. 0-486-27557-4

SANDITON AND THE WATSONS: Austen's Unfinished Novels, Jane Austen. Two tantalizing incomplete stories revisit Austen's customary milieu of courtship and venture into new territory, amid guests at a seaside resort. Both are worth reading for pleasure and study. 112pp. 5⅜ x 8½. 0-486-45793-1

THE SCARLET LETTER, Nathaniel Hawthorne. With stark power and emotional depth, Hawthorne's masterpiece explores sin, guilt, and redemption in a story of adultery in the early days of the Massachusetts Colony. 192pp. 5³⁄₁₆ x 8¼.
0-486-28048-9

THE SEASONS OF AMERICA PAST, Eric Sloane. Seventy-five illustrations depict cider mills and presses, sleds, pumps, stump-pulling equipment, plows, and other elements of America's rural heritage. A section of old recipes and household hints adds additional color. 160pp. 8⅜ x 11. 0-486-44220-9

SELECTED CANTERBURY TALES, Geoffrey Chaucer. Delightful collection includes the General Prologue plus three of the most popular tales: "The Knight's Tale," "The Miller's Prologue and Tale," and "The Wife of Bath's Prologue and Tale." In modern English. 144pp. 5³⁄₁₆ x 8¼. 0-486-28241-4

SELECTED POEMS, Emily Dickinson. Over 100 best-known, best-loved poems by one of America's foremost poets, reprinted from authoritative early editions. No comparable edition at this price. Index of first lines. 64pp. 5³⁄₁₆ x 8¼. 0-486-26466-1

SIDDHARTHA, Hermann Hesse. Classic novel that has inspired generations of seekers. Blending Eastern mysticism and psychoanalysis, Hesse presents a strikingly original view of man and culture and the arduous process of self-discovery, reconciliation, harmony, and peace. 112pp. 5³⁄₁₆ x 8¼. 0-486-40653-9

SKETCHING OUTDOORS, Leonard Richmond. This guide offers beginners step-by-step demonstrations of how to depict clouds, trees, buildings, and other outdoor sights. Explanations of a variety of techniques include shading and constructional drawing. 48pp. 11 x 8¼. 0-486-46922-0

Browse over 9,000 books at www.doverpublications.com

SMALL HOUSES OF THE FORTIES: With Illustrations and Floor Plans, Harold E. Group. 56 floor plans and elevations of houses that originally cost less than $15,000 to build. Recommended by financial institutions of the era, they range from Colonials to Cape Cods. 144pp. 8⅜ x 11. 0-486-45598-X

SOME CHINESE GHOSTS, Lafcadio Hearn. Rooted in ancient Chinese legends, these richly atmospheric supernatural tales are recounted by an expert in Oriental lore. Their originality, power, and literary charm will captivate readers of all ages. 96pp. 5⅜ x 8½. 0-486-46306-0

SONGS FOR THE OPEN ROAD: Poems of Travel and Adventure, Edited by The American Poetry & Literacy Project. More than 80 poems by 50 American and British masters celebrate real and metaphorical journeys. Poems by Whitman, Byron, Millay, Sandburg, Langston Hughes, Emily Dickinson, Robert Frost, Shelley, Tennyson, Yeats, many others. Note. 80pp. 5³⁄₁₆ x 8¼. 0-486-40646-6

SPOON RIVER ANTHOLOGY, Edgar Lee Masters. An American poetry classic, in which former citizens of a mythical midwestern town speak touchingly from the grave of the thwarted hopes and dreams of their lives. 144pp. 5³⁄₁₆ x 8¼.
0-486-27275-3

STAR LORE: Myths, Legends, and Facts, William Tyler Olcott. Captivating retellings of the origins and histories of ancient star groups include Pegasus, Ursa Major, Pleiades, signs of the zodiac, and other constellations. "Classic." — *Sky & Telescope.* 58 illustrations. 544pp. 5⅜ x 8½. 0-486-43581-4

THE STRANGE CASE OF DR. JEKYLL AND MR. HYDE, Robert Louis Stevenson. This intriguing novel, both fantasy thriller and moral allegory, depicts the struggle of two opposing personalities — one essentially good, the other evil — for the soul of one man. 64pp. 5³⁄₁₆ x 8¼. 0-486-26688-5

SURVIVAL HANDBOOK: The Official U.S. Army Guide, Department of the Army. This special edition of the Army field manual is geared toward civilians. An essential companion for campers and all lovers of the outdoors, it constitutes the most authoritative wilderness guide. 288pp. 5³⁄₁₆ x 8¼. 0-486-46184-X

A TALE OF TWO CITIES, Charles Dickens. Against the backdrop of the French Revolution, Dickens unfolds his masterpiece of drama, adventure, and romance about a man falsely accused of treason. Excitement and derring-do in the shadow of the guillotine. 304pp. 5³⁄₁₆ x 8¼. 0-486-40651-2

TEN PLAYS, Anton Chekhov. *The Sea Gull, Uncle Vanya, The Three Sisters, The Cherry Orchard,* and *Ivanov,* plus 5 one-act comedies: *The Anniversary, An Unwilling Martyr, The Wedding, The Bear,* and *The Proposal.* 336pp. 5³⁄₁₆ x 8¼. 0-486-46560-8

THE FLYING INN, G. K. Chesterton. Hilarious romp in which pub owner Humphrey Hump and friend take to the road in a donkey cart filled with rum and cheese, inveighing against Prohibition and other "oppressive forms of modernity." 320pp. 5⅜ x 8½. 0-486-41910-X

THIRTY YEARS THAT SHOOK PHYSICS: The Story of Quantum Theory, George Gamow. Lucid, accessible introduction to the influential theory of energy and matter features careful explanations of Dirac's anti-particles, Bohr's model of the atom, and much more. Numerous drawings. 1966 edition. 240pp. 5⅜ x 8½. 0-486-24895-X

TREASURE ISLAND, Robert Louis Stevenson. Classic adventure story of a perilous sea journey, a mutiny led by the infamous Long John Silver, and a lethal scramble for buried treasure — seen through the eyes of cabin boy Jim Hawkins. 160pp. 5³⁄₁₆ x 8¼.
0-486-27559-0

THE TRIAL, Franz Kafka. Translated by David Wyllie. From its gripping first sentence onward, this novel exemplifies the term "Kafkaesque." Its darkly humorous narrative recounts a bank clerk's entrapment in a bureaucratic maze, based on an undisclosed charge. 176pp. 5³⁄₁₆ x 8¼. 0-486-47061-X

THE TURN OF THE SCREW, Henry James. Gripping ghost story by great novelist depicts the sinister transformation of 2 innocent children into flagrant liars and hypocrites. An elegantly told tale of unspoken horror and psychological terror. 96pp. 5³⁄₁₆ x 8¼. 0-486-26684-2

UP FROM SLAVERY, Booker T. Washington. Washington (1856-1915) rose to become the most influential spokesman for African-Americans of his day. In this eloquently written book, he describes events in a remarkable life that began in bondage and culminated in worldwide recognition. 160pp. 5³⁄₁₆ x 8¼. 0-486-28738-6

VICTORIAN HOUSE DESIGNS IN AUTHENTIC FULL COLOR: 75 Plates from the "Scientific American – Architects and Builders Edition," 1885-1894, Edited by Blanche Cirker. Exquisitely detailed, exceptionally handsome designs for an enormous variety of attractive city dwellings, spacious suburban and country homes, charming "cottages" and other structures — all accompanied by perspective views and floor plans. 80pp. 9¼ x 12¼. 0-486-29438-2

VILLETTE, Charlotte Brontë. Acclaimed by Virginia Woolf as "Brontë's finest novel," this moving psychological study features a remarkably modern heroine who abandons her native England for a new life as a schoolteacher in Belgium. 480pp. 5³⁄₁₆ x 8¼. 0-486-45557-2

THE VOYAGE OUT, Virginia Woolf. A moving depiction of the thrills and confusion of youth, Woolf's acclaimed first novel traces a shipboard journey to South America for a captivating exploration of a woman's growing self-awareness. 288pp. 5³⁄₁₆ x 8¼. 0-486-45005-8

WALDEN; OR, LIFE IN THE WOODS, Henry David Thoreau. Accounts of Thoreau's daily life on the shores of Walden Pond outside Concord, Massachusetts, are interwoven with musings on the virtues of self-reliance and individual freedom, on society, government, and other topics. 224pp. 5³⁄₁₆ x 8¼. 0-486-28495-6

WILD PILGRIMAGE: A Novel in Woodcuts, Lynd Ward. Through startling engravings shaded in black and red, Ward wordlessly tells the story of a man trapped in an industrial world, struggling between the grim reality around him and the fantasies his imagination creates. 112pp. 6⅛ x 9¼. 0-486-46583-7

WILLY POGÁNY REDISCOVERED, Willy Pogány. Selected and Edited by Jeff A. Menges. More than 100 color and black-and-white Art Nouveau–style illustrations from fairy tales and adventure stories include scenes from Wagner's "Ring" cycle, *The Rime of the Ancient Mariner, Gulliver's Travels,* and *Faust.* 144pp. 8⅜ x 11. 0-486-47046-6

WOOLLY THOUGHTS: Unlock Your Creative Genius with Modular Knitting, Pat Ashforth and Steve Plummer. Here's the revolutionary way to knit — easy, fun, and foolproof! Beginners and experienced knitters need only master a single stitch to create their own designs with patchwork squares. More than 100 illustrations. 128pp. 6½ x 9¼. 0-486-46084-3

WUTHERING HEIGHTS, Emily Brontë. Somber tale of consuming passions and vengeance — played out amid the lonely English moors — recounts the turbulent and tempestuous love story of Cathy and Heathcliff. Poignant and compelling. 256pp. 5³⁄₁₆ x 8¼. 0-486-29256-8

Browse over 9,000 books at www.doverpublications.com

Table of Contents

Words in **boldface** type in the text are defined
in the Glossary in the back of this book.

Chapter 1

The Sports Car

Most cars are for everyday use. A few cars, though, are driven just for excitement. They are sports cars.

The word "sport" is used a lot in naming cars. You have probably seen the letters SS and GS on cars. SS stands for sports **sedan**. GS stands for grand sport.

Because the word "sport" is used so often, it is hard to say what a sports car really is. But there are a few things a sports car is not. It is not made for fuel economy. It is not made to hold extra passengers or loads like a van or a

Sports car makers want their cars to look fast.

station wagon. It is not made for comfort like a sedan.

A sports car is designed for the fun of driving. It usually has only two seats. A sports car is exciting to drive.

Power, Handling, and Styling

Power, handling, and styling are the measures of a sports car. A car maker must balance these elements when putting together a sports car.

A big engine might provide a lot of power but it might be heavy. Then the weight of the engine works against the power. A lighter engine with a little less power might perform better.

Handling means how a car performs on the road. A good sports car takes corners well. It hugs the road. The rear end does not **fishtail** easily. The car does not vibrate at high speeds.

Sports cars are sleek and appealing on the inside as well as the outside.

The steering is **responsive**, not slow and heavy.
The car is not likely to **oversteer**.

Styling is the look of the car inside and out.
Sports car makers want their cars to look fast.
They give the cars sleek and appealing bodies.
They try hard to make the cars look different
from other cars.

10

Most sports cars have only two seats.

The low front and smooth lines of a sports car are exciting to look at. They also make the car **aerodynamic**. The shape of the car cuts through the wind. That makes the car go faster.

Chapter 2
History

The term "sports car" was used as early as 1900. The Sports Motor Car Company of London, England, made a two-**cylinder** car that averaged 35 miles (56 kilometers) per hour. That was considered fast at the time. By 1910, 46 different car makers were making some kind of sports car.

Many of the early sports cars are **collectibles**. They are worth a lot of money. Some new cars even sell for more than a car

Porsche is one of the great names in sports cars. The name comes from Dr. Ferdinand Porsche of Austria.

The rare Duesenberg is worth more than $1 million.

maker is asking. The buyers think the car will become a collectible one day.

Type 35 and Duesenberg

The Type 35 is one of the oldest collectible cars. It was made by Bugatti of Italy. The car came out in 1924. It had a **straight eight-**cylinder engine. That means eight cylinders are set in a straight row. It was built both as a racing car and a sports car.

Duesenberg made a special two-seater car in 1934 in Indianapolis. It was a sleek luxury car. Only two were made. Today, the cars are worth more than $1 million each.

Concept Cars

Sports cars often start as **concept cars**. These cars are usually one-of-a-kind. They are built so car makers can try out new ideas. Sometimes they do not even have working engines. They are sent to auto shows so manufacturers can see how people like them.

Sometimes concept cars are big hits at shows. If people like a concept car, a car maker might decide to manufacture the car and sell it to the general public.

This is what happened in 1953 with the Chevrolet Corvette. It also happened in 1989 with the Dodge Viper. These popular cars started out as concept cars.

Chapter 3
Exotic Imports

There have been many important sports car makers over the years. Alfa Romeo, Ferrari, and Maserati are famous sports car makers from Italy. Triumph, Jaguar, and MG are famous British car makers. Interesting cars have also been built in Germany, Sweden, France, and Japan.

Porsche

Porsche is one of the great names in sports cars. The name comes from Dr. Ferdinand Porsche of Austria. He was one of the makers of the Volkswagen in the 1930s.

The basic shape of Porsches has been the same for years.

He created a new type of racing car in 1933 called the P-wagen. The engine was in the back of the car, behind the driver. The P-wagen had a huge **V-16** engine.

After World War II, Dr. Porsche's son, Ferry Porsche, formed a company that produced the modern Porsche sports car. It was based on the Volkswagen. It had a rear-mounted four-cylinder engine.

Enzo Ferrari started his sports car company in 1940.

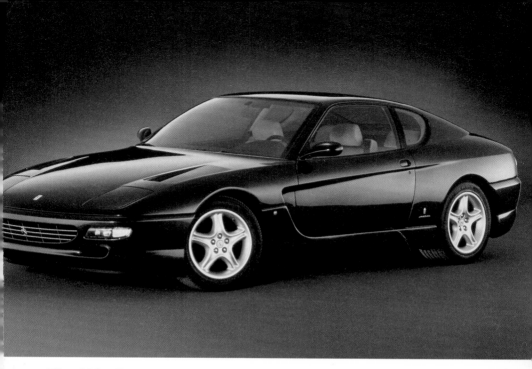

The 1995 Ferrari 456GT has a rare six-speed transmission.

That first car was made in 1949. It was called the Porsche 356. The basic shape of the car remained the same for years.

The 911

The Porsche 911 was first made in 1963. It had a top speed of 124 miles (198 kilometers) per hour. The 911 was hard to handle. It was unstable on corners because the rear of the car was very heavy.

In 1989, the 911 was redesigned. The redesigned 911 could go 163 miles (261 kilometers) per hour. **Four-wheel drive** helped keep the car on the road.

Today, the Porsche 911 has the same classic curvy lines it had in 1963. The 1996 model has a top speed of 168 miles (269 kilometers) per hour.

Ferrari

Enzo Ferrari started his own sports car company in 1940 in Italy. It did not last long. When Italy entered World War II the same year, sports car production stopped. Everyone put their efforts into fighting the war. But soon after the war ended in 1945, Ferrari was back to work.

In 1946, he built a two-seater with a 12-cylinder engine. The car became known as the Barchetta. Barchetta means little boat in

In 1949, the Ferrari Barchetta won the famous 24-hour race at LeMans. Since then, Ferraris have been famous around the world.

The Barchetta had a 12-cylinder engine.

Italian. It got the name because the body surrounded the driver like a speedboat.

In 1949, the Barchetta won the famous 24-hour Le Mans race in France. Ferrari became famous around the world. Ferraris have been one of the top sports cars ever since.

The 1995 Ferrari 456GT had a **V-12** aluminum engine. It had a rare six-speed transmission. Most cars have four- or five-speed transmissions.

Ferrari engineers said the car had a top speed of 190 miles (304 kilometers) per hour. When tested, though, the 456GT went only 175 miles (280 kilometers) per hour. Still, that was fast enough to beat just about everyone else.

Mazda Miata

Mazda of Japan introduced the Miata in 1990. It created a stir. The Miata had smooth, rounded, simple lines. It looked a little like the old Ferrari Barchetta.

People liked the change. For years and years, sports cars had sharp edges. The Miata was different.

It had a four-cylinder engine mounted in front. The Miata was not a fast sports cars. But that was not the point. It handled well and hugged the road. It was fun and exciting to drive.

The first Miatas were huge sellers. A lot of drivers wanted one, not just sports car fans. Prices quickly went higher than Mazda had originally asked. People thought the car would become a collectible. The Miata is still a popular car.

Chapter 4

Muscle Cars

U p until the early 1950s, car makers in the United States had no cars to rival the speedy and stylish European models. Then, in the 1960s, U.S. manufacturers began to make sports cars that are known today as muscle cars.

These were cars with big engines. They were made to perform like race cars, though they were sold to the public to use on regular roads.

Carroll Shelby worked with Ford to make an exciting Mustang called the GT 350.

Chevrolet Corvette

Chevrolet made the first Corvette in 1953. It is the oldest American sports car. The first Corvette looked like a sports car. The body panels were unusual. They were made of fiberglass instead of metal.

The first Corvette did not act like a sports car, though. Most of its parts were the same as the ones used in standard Chevrolet sedans.

It had a 150-horsepower **straight six**-cylinder engine. The engine was called the Blue Flame. It had a two-speed **automatic transmission**. No true sports car of the time had an automatic transmission. The Corvette took more than 11 seconds to go from zero to 60 miles (96 kilometers) per hour. It was a slowpoke.

The V-8

In 1955, the Corvette was made with its first **V-8** engine. By 1956, the Corvette went from zero to 60 miles (96 kilometers) per hour in under eight seconds.

The first Corvettes were slowpokes.

In races at Daytona Beach, Florida, Betty Skelton drove her Corvette 138 miles (221 kilometers) per hour. Her teammate, John Fitch, pushed his Corvette to 146 miles (234 kilometers) per hour. Fitch's speed was the fastest on the track.

The Corvette raced in Europe against cars made by Mercedes, Ferrari, Jaguar, and Porsche. The races helped build worldwide respect for the Corvette.

The Sting Ray

The next big step came in 1963 when Chevy rolled out the Corvette Sting Ray. It featured a sharper front and back. The headlights disappeared into the hood when they were turned off. This feature was unusual at the time.

There was a narrow divider between two rear windows. It was called a backbone. The backbone was dropped after the first year. Because the backbone is so rare, the 1963 Sting Ray is one of the most collectible Corvettes.

The 1963 Sting Ray is collectible because of the backbone.

Other Corvettes

In 1968, the lines of the Corvette grew even sharper. The new body design was based on a concept car called the Mako Shark.

In 1970, a 454 cubic inch (7,446 cubic centimeters) engine was offered as an option. It was the biggest Corvette engine so far.

Soon after the 454 was offered, the ZL-1 Corvette was made. It had an aluminum engine and more than 500 horsepower. Only two ZL-1s were built.

From 1973 to 1982, the Corvette had a bad reputation. Drivers complained of rough handling. There were squeaks from body panels that did not fit together well.

New Design

Because of the complaints, Chevy redesigned the Corvette in 1983. The redesigned Corvette was a 1984 model. There never was a 1983 model Corvette.

The 1984 Corvette was lighter, roomier, and quicker than earlier models. It went from zero to 60 miles (96 kilometers) per hour in 4.8

The Corvette is the oldest American sports car.

seconds. It was a big improvement over its 1953 ancestor.

The 1995 Corvette came with either an LT1 engine or an optional ZR-1 engine. The LT1 delivered a top speed of 161 miles (258 kilometers) per hour. The ZR-1 reached 179 miles (286 kilometers) per hour.

But the ZR-1 cost almost twice as much as the LT1. Sales of the ZR-1 were low. Chevrolet stopped making it the same year it was introduced.

Interest in both new and old Corvettes is strong. **Road rallies** and auto shows keep Corvette lovers busy and happy. There are Corvette clubs all over the world.

Ford Thunderbird

To compete with the Corvette, Ford made a two-seater sports car called the Thunderbird in 1955. Buyers could choose either a removable hardtop roof or a soft-top convertible roof. The convertible roof had to be put down by hand.

The Ford Mustang was introduced at the New York World's Fair in 1964.

The first hardtops featured small porthole windows on the sides. Today, these cars are collectibles. They are often called T-birds.

The T-bird did not remain a sports car for long. The car became a four-seater in 1958. More changes followed. The Thunderbird name was stuck on cars that grew bigger and bigger.

By the 1970s, the Thunderbird was a huge sedan. The Thunderbird is still produced, but it

The Mustang has remained popular since it was introduced.

is nothing like the unusual sports car of the 1950s.

Ford Mustang

The Ford Mustang was introduced at the New York World's Fair in 1964. It did not have the aerodynamic look of the Corvette. Its boxy rear end made it look different than most cars of the time. But the Mustang was very popular.

Shelby Cars

A car designer named Carroll Shelby is a legend in the world of high-performance cars. In 1961, he put a small Ford V-8 engine into a British roadster to create the first Shelby Cobra. This car was followed by the more powerful Shelby Cobra 427 in 1965. The Cobra topped out at 134 miles (214 kilometers) per hour.

In 1965, Shelby worked with Ford to make an exciting Mustang called the GT 350. Later, he made the GT 500.

Shelby cars are collectibles. They were never meant to be road cars. They were built as race cars. They were only sold as road cars to qualify them for certain races.

Chapter 5

The Dodge Viper RT/10

In 1988, Chrysler built a concept car inspired by the 1965 Shelby Cobra. It was a risky project because Chrysler was in bad financial shape.

Carroll Shelby was a member of the design team. The new car was the Viper. It was displayed on the 1989 auto show circuit.

The Viper was a tremendous hit. Like the Cobra, the Viper was a basic sports car. It had two seats. It had a soft-top convertible roof. It had a **manual transmission**.

The Viper was inspired by the 1965 Shelby Cobra.

Modern Technology

But the Viper was not just an updated copy of
the Cobra. It was built with modern technology.
Engineers used computers to design the
suspension. The engine is based on a Chrysler
10-cylinder truck engine. It was made from
aluminum by Lamborghini, a famous car maker
from Italy.

The **urethane** foam interior trim provides
extra support. The body is made from RTM, a

The Viper is for people who want a thrilling ride in a beautiful machine.

kind of fiberglass. RTM stands for resin transfer molding.

Demand

Sports car lovers went crazy over the Viper concept car. Some of them even sent in money to reserve a new car. But Chrysler had no plans to put the Viper in production. Chrysler sent the money back.

Eventually, the demand became so great that the company could not resist. On December 9, 1991, the first production Viper rolled out of Chrysler's factory in Detroit. It was the 1992 Dodge Viper RT/10. Only 200 were made.

Demand was so strong that some buyers made bids four times higher than the price Chrysler was asking for the car.

The Production Model

The 1992 Viper had a 488 cubic inch (8,003 cubic centimeter) **V-10** engine. It ran from zero

The Viper drives like a race car.

to 60 miles (96 kilometers) per hour in 4.6 seconds. In one test, it hit 163 miles (261 kilometers) per hour and still was not in the top gear.

The Viper drives like a race car. The steering is responsive. But with all that power, it tends to oversteer while cornering. The driver's skill has to match the Viper's challenge.

The Viper is for people who want a thrilling drive in a beautiful machine. They have to be willing to give up some comfort for it. The interior gets hot. There is no extra room to

move around. Drivers have to stop the car to put on plastic window flaps by hand. But for sports car lovers, that is all part of the sports car experience.

Future Vipers

The 1996 Viper was the first model with roll-up windows. Some sports car lovers

The 1996 Viper was the first model with roll-up windows.

wonder what the Viper will look like in 20 years. They want to know if the roll-up windows are the start of more changes. Some people fear that the Viper will be tamed like the Thunderbird was. They hope Chrysler will stay true to the sports car the way Chevrolet did with the Corvette.

Glossary

aerodynamic—designed to cut down on wind resistance

automatic transmission—gears that shift without assistance from the driver

collectible—an item that increases in value over time, like an antique

concept cars—vehicles built to show off an idea

cylinder—can-shaped area of an engine that holds the pistons where gas is ignited

fishtail—the swerving back and forth of a car's back end

four-wheel drive—special feature that allows an engine to turn all four wheels, not just the two back wheels

manual transmission—gears that a driver must shift by hand

oversteer—the tendency of a car to turn too much, causing it to slip sideways or to fishtail

responsive—when a car reacts easily to steering and acceleration

road rallies—gatherings of cars for a trip or a race on public roads

sedan—a hardtop car with two or four doors and a front and rear seat

straight eight—an engine with eight cylinders set in a straight row

straight six—an engine with six cylinders set in a straight row

suspension—the system of springs and shocks that supports a vehicle

urethane—special, strong chemical compound

V-8—an engine with eight cylinders set in pairs at angle that form the shape of a "V"

V-16—an engine with 16 cylinders set in pairs at angle that form the shape of a "V"

V-10—an engine with 10 cylinders set in pairs at angle that form the shape of a "V"

V-12—an engine with 12 cylinders set in pairs at angle that form the shape of a "V"

To Learn More

Holder, William G. and Phillip Kunz. *American Muscle Cars.* New York: Tab Books, 1992.

Leffingwell, Randy. *Porsche Legends.* Osceola, Wis.: Motorbooks International, 1992.

Merskey, Jane. *Exotic Cars.* Mankato, Minn.: Crestwood House, 1987.

Royston, Angela. *Cars.* New York: Aladdin Books, 1991.

You can read more about sports cars in *Vette Vues* and *Corvette Enthusiast's Magazine*.

Useful Addresses

Ferrari Club of America
825 Erie Street
Chicago, IL 60622-5904

Fifty 567 Club
2021 Wiggins Avenue
Saskatoon, SK S7J 1W2
Canada

Porsche Club of America
801 Emerson Street
Wichita, KS 67212-3111

Shelby American Auto Club
P.O. Box 788
Sharon, CT 06060-0788

Thunderbirds of America
P.O. Box 2766
Cedar Rapids, IA 52406-2766

Index